# Learning Environments for Young Children

## Rethinking Library Spaces and Services

SANDRA FEINBERG | JOAN F. KUCHNER | SARI FELDMAN

**AMERICAN LIBRARY ASSOCIATION**

Chicago and London

1998

While extensive effort has gone into ensuring the reliability of information appearing in this book, the publisher makes no warranty, express or implied, on the accuracy or reliability of the information, and does not assume and hereby disclaims any liability to any person for any loss or damage caused by errors or omissions in this publication.

Project editor: Louise D. Howe

Cover and text design by Todd Sanders

Composition by The Publishing Services Group in Garamond and Stone Sans typefaces using QuarkXPress 3.32 on a PowerPC.

Printed on 50-pound Finch Opaque, a pH-neutral stock, and bound in 10-point coated cover stock by Edwards Brothers

The paper used in this publication meets the minimum requirements of American National Standard for Information Sciences—Permanence of Paper for Printed Library Materials, ANSI Z39.48-1992. ∞

**Library of Congress Cataloging-in-Publication Data**

Feinberg, Sandra, 1946–
    Learning environments for young children : rethinking library spaces and services / by Sandra Feinberg, Joan F. Kuchner, Sari Feldman.
       p.  cm.
    Includes bibliographical references and index.
    ISBN 0-8389-0736-9
    1. Children's libraries—United States.   2. Libraries and education—United States.   3. Library architecture—United States. I. Kuchner, Joan F.  II. Feldman, Sari, 1953–  .  III. Title.
Z718.2.U6F45   1998
027.62'5'0973—dc21                      98-15275

Printed in the United States of America.

02  01  00  99  98     5  4  3  2  1

*This book is dedicated to our families:*
*Richie, Jake, and Ted Feinberg,*
*Sam and Nettie Feinberg;*
*Eugene, Marc, and Eric Kuchner,*
*Harriet and Howard Freedman; and*
*Matt, Meg, and Bridget O'Dwyer,*
*Minnie and Seymour Feldman,*
*who provided us with the inspiration*
*and support that was needed to*
*create our book.*

# CONTENTS

# FOREWORD

You have in your hands an important book. At the very least, reading it should subtly alter the way you conceptualize library work with children. It is quite possible, however, that this book will dramatically change the way you plan, implement, and evaluate children's services.

In this text, Feinberg, Kuchner, and Feldman have tackled two of the most important questions facing children's librarians: What is our intent in providing services for young children? and How do we know when we are successful?

To answer the first question, they have considered the educational implications and underpinnings of librarianship. As a former children's librarian and a current library educator, I often ask myself and my students: What business are we in? In this book you will find the resounding response: We are in the business of helping children develop. We aid in that development not only with books and programs but with physical environments, with social interactions, with understanding and supportive responses to children, parents, and caregivers, with collaborative ventures, with the entire sum of our efforts.

The authors go on to suggest that we assess the success of our efforts qualitatively rather than in traditional and exclusively quantitative terms. Assessing quality of service is an exciting yet anxiety-ridden undertaking. It is also an undertaking long overdue.

I have not had the pleasure of making Joan's acquaintance, but I recall vividly my first meeting with Sandy and Sari. It occurred during ALA's 1995 Annual Conference in Chicago.

Sue Nespeca had invited the pair to discuss their preliminary work on the early childhood quality review at the Preschool Services Discussion Group. Attendance was particularly large that day and we were all so excited by the ideas Sandy and Sari were expressing that by the close of the session virtually everyone in the group eagerly volunteered to participate in the field study—never mind that no volunteers were needed! That particular day Sandy and Sari found themselves in a room full of librarians eager to consider quality and to assess their work in a more complex fashion than the "numbers game" would allow. I am sure that the members of that discussion group will welcome the chance to see and implement the quality review that Sandy and Sari previewed that day. I am equally sure that they will be joined by countless others ready to create a culture of reflection and assessment among the ranks of children's librarians.

I hope that you are one of those librarians. If you are, I wish you an engaging and thought-provoking read. As a result of your reading, I feel sure that the young children using your library will enjoy a carefully crafted array of services that are thoughtfully implemented and regularly and reflectively reviewed. Children deserve nothing less.

VIKI ASH-GEISLER,
Texas Woman's University

# ACKNOWLEDGMENTS

Special acknowledgment is given to all of the participants and supporters who have made this book possible either through their involvement in the *Early Childhood Quality Review Initiative for Public Libraries* (ECQR) or as personal mentors and advisors in the field of early childhood education and library science.

Appreciation is extended to those professionals who participated in an intensive three-day early childhood institute where the initial adaptation of the *School Quality Review Initiative* began our journey in the development of the ECQR. These participants, listed with their respective libraries, include Sharon Breen and Barbara Jordan, Middle Country (Centereach); Kathleen Cronin, New Rochelle; Kathleen Deerr, Mastic-Moriches-Shirley; Ruth Dorogi, Ahira Hall Memorial; Silvia G. Macor, Rosalind NaPier, and Elizabeth A. Williams, Onondaga County (Syracuse); Rachel Fox, Port Washington; Nancy A. Gifford, Schenectady County; Cassandra B. Hamm, NYS Library for the Blind and Visually Handicapped; Barbara Haymann-Diaz, Greater Poughkeepsie; Sharon Y. Holley, Buffalo & Erie County; James Karge, Crandall (Glens Falls); Michele Lauer-Bader, Patchogue Medford; Jane Marino, Scarsdale; Leslie Nover, Saratoga Springs; Ellen Riboldi, Great Neck; Patricia Roos, Manhasset; Marilyn Schoenblum, Yonkers; Carolyn Schuler, Monroe County (Rochester); and Margaret Tice, Brooklyn.

Special recognition is extended to the Loleta D. Fyan Grant, American Library Association, that provided partial funding for the initial draft of the ECQR. Mary Jo Lynch, ALA Office for Research and Statistics, was particularly helpful and supportive throughout the process. Recognition is given to the New York State Department of Education, which funded the Institute during the summer of 1994 and provided a two-day training to our field site libraries during the fall of 1995. Particular thanks are extended to Roseanne DeFabio, Edith Toohey, Thomas Fitzgerald, and Paula Barry, NYS Department of Education; Elaine Frankonis, Cultural Education Center; and Anne Simon, Division of Library Development.

Sincere appreciation is extended to the staffs and families from the Mastics-Moriches-Shirley Community Library, Middle Country Public Library, Newburgh Public Library, Patchogue Medford Library and Shoreham Wading River (North Shore) Public Library who participated in the field testing of the ECQR. Special thanks to Mary Schumacher, Sharon Breen, Barbara Jordan, Ellen Friedman, and Rochelle Lipkind from the Middle Country Public Library for their leadership and management of the regional implementation of the field testing. Recognition is given to the Child and Family Studies students from the State University of New York at Stony Brook who participated in the field testing. Particular thanks to student Jane O'Brien who contributed her time and expertise to the Middle Country Team. The time and commitment to the field testing exhibited by all the participants were exemplary. Recog-nition for partial funding of the field testing goes to the New York State Parent and Child Grants.

Acknowledgment is extended to our personal supporters and colleagues: the staff and board of the Middle Country Public Library, particularly Rochelle Lipkind, Assistant Director; Daniel G. Freedman, Professor Emeritus, Department of Psychology and the Committee on Human Development, University of Chicago; the faculty and staff of the Social Science Interdisciplinary Program, SUNY at Stony Brook including Dr. Beverly Birns, Dr. Barbara Baskin, Dr. Eli Seifman, Dr. Shi Ming Hu, Dr. George Fouron, Dr. Judy Wishnia, Dr. Marie Fitzgerald, Anne Raybin, Denise Masone, and Vera Baquet; Lucille Oddo, Executive Director, Stony Brook Child Care Service Inc. and her staff; the staff of the Cleveland Public Library; and the staff of the Onondaga County Public Library (Syracuse, N.Y.).

# Introduction

Since the early 1900s librarians have been increasing their focus on serving children. Now more than ever the work of the children's librarian and service to young children have reached critical proportion. Scientific advances have repeatedly confirmed the importance of early experience on brain development in humans.* As this information reaches the public's attention and captures their imagination, there has been a renewed interest in the importance of learning during the early childhood years. Armed with scientific documentation, libraries have a new rationale for examining essential roles to satisfy the learning needs of infants, toddlers, and preschoolers, as well as their parents and caregivers.

No umbrella program or government mandate has established clear models of service for the entire birth through eight age group. In this environment, librarians have an opportunity to position themselves as vital participants and leaders in the education of infants and young children, their parents, and other caregivers.

*Learning Environments for Young Children: Rethinking Library Spaces and Services* provides the foundation and infrastructure for understanding developmentally appropriate practice and family centered principles in the library context and uses this vision for expanding ideas about library service for infants, young children, and their families. Based on research, adaptations from related disciplines, and the field testing of a draft review process, the text evolved as a collaborative process. It draws on the combined expertise of public library administrators with experience in developing and evaluating model

---

*Evidence from positive emission tomography (PET) has documented that the years from birth to age three are essential for brain development, particularly the establishment and growth of connections between nerves. Those areas of the brain that are stimulated by sensory and perceptual activity thrive and expand, while those neural pathways that do not receive stimulation are already being eliminated. Connections that are critical for language development and that provide the foundation for the development of math and logic are formed beginning in infancy (Snow 1998).

programs for young children and families (Sandra Feinberg and Sari Feldman) and a developmental psychologist and professor of child and family studies who specializes in infancy and early childhood, parenting, and play and environment issues (Joan F. Kuchner, Ph.D.).

# THE ROLE OF THE LIBRARY

Today's public librarian is grappling with diminishing resources and technological change. Having to compete for public dollars forces libraries into competition with other educational, social service, and health-related institutions as well as private business and other not-for-profit and profit-oriented agencies. By reviewing and evaluating services, librarians can effectively develop a quality library-based learning environment for young children and compete professionally in the early childhood education marketplace.

It is critical to broaden the perception of librarians as early childhood and family support service providers and to provide a method for encouraging the provision of high-quality services. Through critical self-evaluation, libraries have an opportunity to play a vital role in the educational process for children from birth through age eight, acting in full partnership with other community agencies that serve families and young children. *Learning Environments for Young Children: Rethinking Library Spaces and Services* offers a means to respond to these social realities.

While in the past half-century demand prompted the increase in library-based early childhood services, in the twenty-first century it must be quality that strengthens and enhances these services. The economic realities make this move imperative. *Learning Environments for Young Children* provides the background information, logical analysis, and quality-assurance tools to enable libraries to take a leadership position in the provision of services for infants, young children, and their families. The creation of environments, collections, services, and programs targeted to young children, their families, and the professionals who work with and for them needs to be given top priority. The time is right for libraries to bridge the gap in service delivery and to weave connections between existing library programs and community services. Libraries have the opportunity to define and lead the community toward quality early childhood learning.

# LIBRARIANS AS TEACHERS

While children's librarians generally find it easy to define their work as supporting parents and other professionals, particularly early childhood and parent educators, many become uncomfortable talking about their direct work with children within the context of education. In the summer of 1994, twenty-three children's librarians from around New York State came together to discuss the role of the librarian as an educator and to initiate the development of a library-based early childhood quality review process.

One of the first orders of business was to consider the notions of teaching and learning in public libraries, particularly the librarian's role in working with young children and their families. During this discussion the word "teaching" caused the greatest reactions from participant librarians. Many saw a clear distinction between their role and that of an elementary school or early childhood teacher. However, just as the teaching profession has embraced discovery, facilitated, and cooperative learning, these librarians began to shift their thinking and discovered similarities between library work and the work of classroom teachers.

Brainstorming among the participants produced a list of words that describe the teaching and learning that occurs in public libraries. Facilitated learning, client-centered learning, pre-reading skills development, love of literature, parent/child learning and family-centered learning were among the phrases librarians used to define their daily work. Other phrases that the librarians used to capture the essence of children's services included use of motivational techniques, building self-esteem, letter/word/number recognition, integration of skills and instruction, active listening, reading readiness, provision of role models, developmentally appropriate practice, and holistic approach. Together, the twenty-three children's librarians developed a common understanding of their teaching role in the learning environment of a public library.

The following year, five public libraries participated as test sites for the *Early Childhood Quality Review Initiative for Public Libraries* (1995), expanding upon observations of the library as a learning center and the librarian as a learning facilitator. Some of the most exciting examples provided by this group describe the skill building that can occur for children over a series of library programs. This documented the longitudinal impact of the learning environment for children and families created in public libraries.

Just as this small group of New York State librarians was wrestling with the role of the librarian as learning facilitator, the American Library Association was embracing the idea that "learning begins before schooling." In light of the National Education Goals, the American Library Association as well as leaders in the library field began to emphasize the role of the public library both as a learning environment in its own right and as a support for parents, early childhood educators, and professionals (Immroth and Ash-Geisler 1995; *Kids Need Libraries* 1991).

## THE CHANGING PROGRAM ENVIRONMENT

Trends in national education and new scientific evidence are facilitating a new dialog for children's librarians which offers an opportunity for fundamental change. Quality library-based programs and services for young children and their parents must be developed and delivered by skilled library staff. Policies and practices for early childhood services in libraries must build upon the knowledge and understanding of developmentally appropriate behaviors and family centered principles.

The vision of facilitated learning by children, families, and the community is based on the idea that all children can learn and are entitled to equitable access to cognitively enriching, socio-emotionally satisfying, and developmentally appropriate resources and learning opportunities. It will be realized in the public library setting when:

- The public library offers a community-based educational setting in which librarians function as educators, guides, coaches, and facilitators of active learning throughout the life cycle.

- Libraries provide diverse collections, programs, and technical resources for young children, parents, and adults who work with families and recognize and support parents as the child's first and best teachers.

- Libraries build on family strengths and offer learning opportunities that reflect the interests, cultures, and needs of young children and their families.

- The library environment ensures a nonjudgmental, integrated, and interdisciplinary approach to lifelong learning that fosters the development of the whole person, whether child or adult.

- The diverse array of accessible collections, services, programs, and technical resources fosters a child's focused participation, creativity, critical thinking ability, cooperation, and problem-solving skills and supports the concept of self-motivated lifelong learning that ensures both children and adults the expectations of success.

The underlying philosophy of *Learning Environments for Young Children* is that libraries are and should be offering services for young children and their families. The critical issues are how best to provide these services in the library setting and how best to present the educational role of the library to the public and to the professional community. To be recognized as full partners, librarians need to examine their practices, competencies, and standards not only in relationship to the field of early childhood but also in relationship to other education, health and human service disciplines.

The book is divided into three sections. The first section offers an overview of theory and practice in building developmentally appropriate and family centered social and physical environments that recognize the contributions of parents as partners. Secondary themes deal with the importance of continued education, professional development, and the creation and maintenance of professional and personal networks throughout life. The book identifies the leadership roles of librarians and library administrators in shaping the environment to address the needs of young children, to support adults in their parenting roles, and to develop collaborations with community agencies. By acting as advocates both within the library and throughout the greater community, librarians can build a community that nurtures and supports lifelong learning from birth.

The second section of the book emphasizes the importance of establishing a culture of review in order to gain a greater understanding of early childhood services within the library. It outlines a self-review process, from inspiration through data collection and the development of a collective perspective, that leads to new short-term actions and strategic plans. Alternative techniques for gathering and analyzing information about the impact of the social and physical environment, the nature of teaching and learning, the participation of parents, the range of community collaborations, the distribution of resources, the encouragement of professional development, and the perception of the children's programs within the community are presented. A range of observational and interview methodologies suitable for library environments is described and techniques for gathering and analyzing library documents and communications are presented.

The third section of the book provides replicable forms for guiding discussion, recording observations, and summarizing documentation. These are coordinated with the core elements presented earlier and grouped by methodological strategies.

# The Audience

Although *Learning Environments for Young Children* is primarily directed to actively practicing librarians, library staff, and administrators, it addresses significant issues about the nature of early childhood places and programs that are relevant to all community professionals who work with young children and families, irrespective of their affiliation. This book provides a model of self-review that could easily be adapted for other specialized locations and institutions as different as social services, museums, and clinical medical practices. It has potential to be used as a stimulating text for the education and training of librarians and of early childhood and social service professionals. Early childhood and elementary teachers and administrators, early intervention specialists, and community leaders will all find something useful in its pages, as it provides cogent arguments for professional development and offers ideas for creative collaborations and networking. Certain chapters offer excellent resources and ideas for architects, city planners, environmental psychologists, and commercial businesses. Part One offers relevant and detailed information on the creation and maintenance of environments for young children, their parents, and other caregivers, while Part Two, which covers the review process itself, is readily applicable to post-occupancy evaluations of other community-based settings targeting young children and their families.

REFERENCES

*The Early Childhood Quality Review Initiative for public libraries.* 1995. Centereach, N.Y.: Middle Country Public Library.

Immroth, B. F., and V. Ash-Geisler, eds. 1995. *Achieving school readiness: Public libraries and national education goal no. 1.* Chicago: American Library Association.

*Kids need libraries: Implementing the national goals for education through library services.* 1991. Chicago: American Library Association.

Snow, C. 1998. *Infant development,* 2nd ed. Upper Saddle River, N.J.: Prentice Hall.

# PART

# I

# Essential Elements for Learning

# Family Centered and Developmentally Appropriate Practice

Quality environments and services for young children are built upon an understanding of human development. All programs for young children that are developmentally appropriate recognize and celebrate the significant role of the family in children's lives. Until now, the exploration and discussion of particular strategies for guiding and interacting with young children and families have been largely contained within the community of early childhood professionals based in schools, child-care centers, and family day-care homes. Young children, however, are not limited in their activities and movements to these locations. Rather, they inhabit a range of public and private educational and recreational settings including museums, malls, playgrounds, restaurants, health-care facilities, and libraries.

With increasing frequency, communities have begun to recognize that public libraries can be safe, supportive sites for the promotion of young children's learning. The library's role in supporting individually paced lifelong learning makes it an ideal location for introducing young children to the pleasures of discovery learning and for nurturing the learning connection between the parent and young child.

More than ever before, developmentally appropriate practices and family centered services and programs belong in public libraries. What do these services look like in a library environment? What is the relationship between librarians and parents? How can early childhood service be designed for public access and consumption? What are the implications of a developmentally appropriate, family centered approach for children's services librarians? The critical issues raised by these questions have profound implications for the design of library services for young children and the creation of a developmentally appropriate, family centered library environment.

# DEVELOPMENTALLY APPROPRIATE PRACTICE

The world of the young child was idealized in the nineteenth century. By the early twentieth century, the emergent field of early childhood education broadly accepted the idea that the minds and feelings of young children were organized in qualitatively different ways than those of older children and adults. However, it was not until 1986, when the National Association for the Education of Young Children came out with its seminal description of developmentally appropriate practice, that this concept began to dominate discussions of acceptable and ideal environments for children.

In order for the child to thrive, the physical setting and the social interactions within that setting must be suitable for the age of the child and right for the particular individual. This premise is basic to the design of developmentally appropriate environments for children. A clear understanding of developmental changes and the relationship of these changes to children's action patterns in public places is the foundation for providing appropriate library-based early childhood programs, spaces, and services.

Creating developmentally appropriate practice requires the understanding that development occurs in a predictable sequence and that there are optimal time periods for the acquisition of particular abilities. Once differentiated, these newly acquired functions recombine to create new patterns of thought and action with each stage creating the base for subsequent development. Within this overall framework, patterns of individual growth, temperament, and interests vary as both biological and environmental factors interact, influencing the child's repertoire of new abilities and skills. This provides an extraordinary window of opportunity for individualized learning. Because development proceeds as an interrelated whole, library environments for infants, toddlers, and young children need to take into account the physical, cognitive, linguistic, emotional, and social capabilities of children.

Contemporary research confirms the view that young children learn most effectively when they are engaged in actively manipulating things. Their understanding of the world and the rules of social interaction is constructed from active engagement and experimentation rather than by being purely passive recipients of information or faithful followers of directions. Teaching and learning in public libraries focus on this type of active exploration and interaction.

Young children in libraries are accompanied by other family members including parents, grandparents, and siblings. Each member of the family network approaches the library with his or her own developmental needs and individual history. These individuals have an impact on how the child perceives and uses the library's services.

Fundamental to developmentally appropriate practice, along with a thorough knowledge of child development and learning, is a respect for children in the context of their family, community, and culture. Each of these groups conveys its own values and priorities to the child and provides access to a different range of settings and opportunities for learning experiences. It is essential to understand that a child's past history shapes his or her current interests and style of interpersonal interaction.

Children are always taking something from their experience. Indeed the issue is not *whether* children are learning, but *what* they are learning about the physical and social world. Matching the content and design of programs and services to the needs, interests, skills, and past histories of individual young children becomes easier once it is recognized that it is the process of noticing, doing, choosing, comparing, and planning that is essential to young children's learning. It is the interactive process, not the end product, that matters at this age.

Throughout the life span, individuals should feel welcome in the library environment and their presence should be valued. Efforts to attain knowledge or information need to be respected and encouraged without placing value judgments on the individual's questions, motivations, or goals. Resources need to be available that take into account individual differences in interest and levels of understanding as well as background knowledge and skills. The physical environment should be arranged to facilitate access to an array of materials and resources while the social environment should facilitate individual exploratory learning and active problem solving. Developmentally appropriate practice supports lifelong learning and assists individuals in defining and reaching their own goals.

# DEVELOPMENTAL REALITIES

## Infants and Toddlers

The demarcation between infancy and toddlerhood is the ability to walk upright. Infants below the age of six months will generally experience the library in the arms of an adult or occasionally an older child. They may see the library from an infant seat or stroller, or while lying on the floor. As infants begin to sit on their own, they are able to reach for objects, pull them toward themselves, and frequently place them in their mouths. Although they cannot easily move from place to place on their own until they begin to roll and crawl, they can gain access to objects and materials from the height of backpacks and strollers. In public libraries, these objects and materials can range from hanging displays to clothing, wires, and protruding books.

Infants accompanying older siblings to the library need a safe place to sit and observe their surroundings. They are interested in strong primary colors, sharp contrasting patterns, and designs that replicate the outlines of the human face. Mirrors are ideal. Proximal communication for infants this age requires physical contact. However, distal communication can take place as the infant uses his or her head and eyes to follow the surrounding action.

Crying is a primary form of communication. As early as five months of age, infants may show a wariness to the presence of strangers. Around eight or nine months they may burst into tears if a stranger ventures too close. These reactions vary with the physical proximity of the parent or primary caregiver, the infant's own temperament, and his or her experience with unfamiliar people and places. Infants take their cues from the reactions of the people around them. This social referencing helps even a seven-month-old interpret whether an action or event is safe. When parents are relaxed and comfortable in the environment, they will convey this feeling to their infants and toddlers.

Infants may not be able to postpone their need for food or comfort easily. They often require feedings or diaper changes during a library visit. A rocking chair can be used to comfort a crying infant or it can be a welcome spot for nursing or feeding a hungry baby. A changing table in a convenient rest room indicates that this is a place where babies' needs are understood.

Infants enjoy a visit to the library not only for the range of sights and sounds but also for the opportunity to interact with books. Toward the end of the first year infants will begin to look at books, magazines, and picture collections. They are able to turn the pages of books with thick pages and some may be interested in pointing out familiar pictures.

By the second half of the first year, infants will respond to the repetition of familiar stories and songs. There is growing evidence that infants will attend to these words and language patterns in other settings. The ritual of reading with an infant contributes to both language learning and a growing sense of trust. Books become connected with the comforting presence of the caregiver. This sense of security and comfort is remembered as the infant interacts with a book independently. For the infant, library experiences can begin to satisfy emotional needs as well as needs for stimulation, building a foundation for positive social interactions and emergent literacy.

During the second half of the first year, major changes occur in the infant's capacity to interact with the environment. Creeping and crawling infants can cover a large area with surprising speed. The months before a toddler's first birthday are marked by increased persistence to attain a destination or object that is initially out of reach. Infants of seven to twelve months are not content to remain in a stroller or seat for extended periods of time. This period of intense motor practice is marked by such developmental milestones as pulling to standing and cruising, using stationary furniture for balance and upright locomotion. Objects and furnishings that are used for support and balance must be sturdy and topple-resistant. Smooth edges and washable surfaces are important for this age group.

Both adults and infants need unobstructed views of each other at all times, even when the infant may seek the apparent privacy of niches or small semi-enclosed areas. Infants who monitor the facial expressions of their primary caregivers acquire important information about behavioral expectations and safety. Toddlers who lose sight of parents or primary caregivers may experience a flood of anxiety surpassing the adult's concern when the infant is momentarily out of view in a safe location. The end of the first year is a particularly sensitive time for infants who are dealing with the emotional issues of separation.

In the transition from crawling to walking, infants will literally gain access to new heights. An average twelve-month-old who is beginning to walk is approximately 29 inches tall, about the height of a standard table or desk. This has implications for both visual sight lines and access to objects, toys, and books.

Toddlers are recognized by the gait that has given its descriptive name to this stage of development. They may walk with their legs spread for balance. Steps are initially negotiated with one foot in the lead. Special care needs to be provided for wide steps to accommodate this type of walk. Toddlers have a high center of gravity compared to older children or adults. A toddler who is poised to look over a railing or edge may be in imminent danger of falling.

Undertaking the task of mastering walking and talking simultaneously results in a wide range of strategies and individual differences. There are numerous examples of normally developing nine- and ten-month-olds whose abilities at upright locomotion and even climbing exceed their ability to stop easily or interrupt their own behavior on request. The ability to follow a command that requires inhibiting or stopping an action in progress is a separate developmental milestone that many children this age have not yet reached.

In general, language comprehension precedes language production so that most toddlers will be able to follow simple positive directions or requests. Directions specifying the desired action will have more positive results than those that attempt to interrupt behavior with "stops" and "don'ts." While toddlers and young children need to know the limits of desired behavior, presenting models and directions of correct or preferred behavior is more effective than repetition of prohibitions.

In the area of language production there is a wide range of variability. While some eighteen-month-olds combine words into strings of two-word utterances, others may have yet to say their first recognizable word. Although children may be surrounded by adult language, their understanding of individual words and sentences does not match adult meanings. They may assign one and only one meaning to a word and be unable to apply it to similar objects. Concepts such as relative size and order are still under construction. Children this age focus on a single dimension or feature of an object or array of objects when applying labels and identifying similarities and differences. Their sense of grouping objects will be based on these frequently superficial and highly visible characteristics. Such connections follow idiosyncratic patterns and are not yet rule based.

This age is characterized by strong emotions as children discover the ability to assert their own preferences. Autonomy for a toddler is associated with the ability to make choices and to do it "myself." It is a time when children may insist on doing things on their own, even though they may still need considerable guidance in how to accomplish the desired end result. Developmentally appropriate practices with this age group include providing a physical and social environment that encourages exploration and individual decision making. Toddlers prefer to make selections by themselves. This means not only selecting a desired book or toy but also being able to reach materials from shelves, containers, and other storage areas.

Toddlers want to be included in the adult world, to see into adult places, and to accomplish adult tasks. Decisions about the physical environment and the development of special programs for this age group need to take into account the important presence of the caregiver as model, guide, and safe base from which the toddler can venture forth into new experiences.

Not all parents and caregivers are equally informed or knowledgeable about the expected behavior for themselves or their children in the library setting. Some adults may assume that it is the librarian's job to monitor and enforce acceptable child behavior. Developing strategies and communication skills to impart the limits and range of acceptable behavior and to emphasize the parent's role in guiding young children toward preferred behavior is critical to the success of library-based early childhood service.

## The Preschool Years

Programs for children throughout the preschool years (ages three to five) need to take into account the importance of physical behavior in a young child's life. Children learn with their entire bodies. For example, concepts acquired through moving in space such as inside and outside, above and below, under and over are critical to the acquisition of related language.

Between the ages of two and three, motor skills that may be initiated in the first year are practiced and coordination is improved. From the perspective of a toddler, steps invite jumping as structures invite climbing. The affordances of the physical environment speak clear messages for action.

Emergent literacy experiences include a kinesthetic response to materials. Through drawing or scribbling, young children discover cause and effect as they begin to notice that their motor action leaves marks on the page. As they approach three, children may see familiar letters in their marks or provide labels for their completed pictures. Young children are also beginning to recognize letters and numbers as different types of symbols, distinct from scribbles and pictures. Providing child-eye-level opportunities to see examples of useful symbols, words, and numbers can enrich the child's experience.

Children may feel conflicting emotions that are difficult to express. Adult validation of the importance of the child's emotions takes place through active listening, book sharing, and participation in play. From the time that children begin to engage in symbolic play (around two years old), play provides an opportunity for children to explore complex emotional ideas.

During the years from three to five, pretend play becomes increasingly important as a vehicle for learning. Through pretend play, children learn about the perspective of others, practice physical coordination, communicate complex emotional ideas, and explore the uses of the printed word. During play, children define their own level of involvement by choosing activities, roles, and companions. This type of self-selection sets the stage for interactions with people and materials that are relevant to their own life. It also provides opportunities for children to learn from each other.

Children take part in mutual imitation around object manipulation and during social interactions. They respond to social overtures and coordinate their words with a partner's action. Social pretend play provides an optimal avenue for acquiring important skills in cooperation and negotiating. It fosters opportunities for children to manipulate words and word meaning through active collaboration.

Although children may at times assert their own needs or establish their proprietary interest in an object or location as a way of initiating a social interaction, some of these self-assertions are not met with success. Adults may need to step in to model negotiating skills in times of conflict. Assisting children may involve helping them find the words that describe the problem or that explore alternative choices for action. Children can then be part of the process of finding appropriate solutions. The public nature of libraries may make it difficult to determine which adult—parent or librarian—should take the initiative in modeling conflict resolution strategies. Creating an environment that facilitates discovery learning in both the physical and social sphere involves using a language of action and words that notices specific behaviors without making value judgments of the whole child.

Three- to five-year-olds may be able to participate in group programs without their parents/caregivers. In order to encourage the discovery process, programs for young children should be designed for small groups and seek to convey ideas through the playful manipulation of relevant materials. For young children, active exploration of physical objects is essential to the internalization of increasingly more complex concepts.

Library programs for this age group provide special opportunities for children to develop self-confidence in taking initiatives and making decisions. They offer social environments that communicate to children that they are valued. Often young children go unrecognized within adult environments. Offering appropriate forums for expression can assist children in exploring and communicating their own reactions and ideas both verbally and nonverbally.

# The Primary Grades

The years from six to eight are also years of rapid cognitive and physical development, even though the rate of physical change appears slower during these years than those that immediately preceded them.

Children six through eight years old still find sitting still for long periods of time more tiring than bouts of physical activity. Concrete direct experiences remain critical to their growing understanding. Despite a greatly expanded vocabulary and more well-defined ability to recognize constancies and rule-governed relationships of things and events, they still derive their most significant learning from testing their ideas against their own perceptions in the physical and social world. Although their mental manipulation of symbols surpasses that of preschool children, six- to eight-year-olds still require hands-on experience both for comprehension and motivation.

The acquisition of social competence requires opportunities to interact with individuals from different backgrounds as well as experiences in various settings and environments. Social behavior and decorum vary in various institutions, neighborhoods, and cultures. Decoding these social arbitrary rules requires practice.

Variations in individual temperament in the areas of sociability, activity, adaptability, persistence, and mood continue to influence how these young children adjust to new environments and people. For some children approaching an unfamiliar adult, such as a librarian, to ask for information or assistance may still require coaching, patience, and encouragement. Success in the social sphere can build confidence that will provide the base for learning in other areas.

## FAMILY CENTERED PRACTICES

Developmentally appropriate practice for infants, toddlers, and young children includes recognizing the importance of parents and family members and incorporating them into program plans and activities. Parents connect with each other in library settings. They begin to view the library as a resource for themselves in their role as parent, as well as in the myriad other roles that they are called upon to assume in the course of a year. Developmentally appropriate services for infants, toddlers, young children, and their parents create lifelong learners. The library can be appreciated as a place where both young children and their parents engage in gathering facts, acquiring skills, building confidence and security, and developing dispositions toward intellectual inquiry and cooperation.

From this vantage point, it is understood that young children will benefit from those places and programs that meet the needs and nurture the skills of the entire family. Families, particularly parents or grandparents as primary caregivers, are the providers of the most significant context in early development. The adage that young children come with families is a daily reality in public libraries.

Family centered principles recognize the pivotal role of the family in the lives of children. A community agency and its staff may provide positive influences in the lives of children. Agencies and staff, however, fluctuate with the geographical location of the family, the age of the child, and the needs of the child. The family is always primary. Service providers from all backgrounds and venues that adopt family centered principles as the underpinning for their work recognize that the role of community institutions is to support families in their natural caregiving roles and to ensure that families are able to collaborate in making decisions regarding their own children. Because families and caregivers accompany young children to the library, librarians have a unique opportunity to integrate family centered principles within early childhood services.

Working with young children in libraries means working with families. Librarians must understand the needs of families for information, education, and recreation. One of the primary life roles for which adults receive little in the way of formal education is parenting. Librarians assist parents in meeting their information needs regarding their child's growth and development and serve to support the parents in their role as the child's primary teachers. They link families to resources within the community, as well as to books, other printed materials, and electronic data. Library services that include parent-child activities and parent education programs and collections provide mechanisms to fulfill the parent's need for parent-to-parent support and foster a partnership between the librarian and the parent.

---

## FAMILY CENTERED PRINCIPLES

* Recognition that the family is the constant in the child's life while the service systems and personnel within those systems fluctuate;

* Facilitation of parent/professional collaboration;

* Sharing of unbiased and complete information with parents about their children on an ongoing basis in an appropriate and supportive manner;

* Implementation of appropriate policies and programs that are comprehensive and provide emotional and financial support to meet the needs of families;

* Encouragement and facilitation of parent-to-parent support;

* Recognition of family strengths and individuality and respect for different methods of coping;

* Assurance that the design of comprehensive, coordinated, multidiscipline service delivery systems is flexible, accessible, and responsive to family identified needs;

* Understanding and incorporating the developmental needs of infants, toddlers, preschoolers, and their families into service delivery systems.

These family centered principles were outlined in the *Surgeon General's Report: Children with Special Health Care Needs, Campaign '87*, adopted by the Association for the Care of Children's Health with support from the Division of Maternal and Child Health, U.S. Public Health Service.

---

Children's librarians have an opportunity to nurture library use. By satisfying the needs of parents and primary caregivers through library service, they begin the process of empowering parents to cultivate this connection for their children. Regular library use by parents to garner information for themselves provides a model of lifelong library use. Adults who are comfortable satisfying their own needs for information in a library will be taking the first step toward motivating their children to seek out library resources for self-discovery, recreation, and educational enrichment. Thus the librarian becomes a guide, one of the most powerful teaching stances for discovery learning.

Effective partnerships extend beyond the family unit to include the development of relationships with adults who work with and for young children and their families. Through networking, cooperative programming, and the building of coalitions and collaborations, community agencies and the library can work to benefit the family unit. Together they can provide a comprehensive approach to satisfy the needs of families within the local community while advocating to effect change at the policy level. Public libraries that promote extensive services for young children and connect with other family support institutions function as models and advocates for developmentally appropriate and family centered practices within the community.

Implementing quality library-based early childhood service requires the integration of family centered principles and developmentally appropriate practice within the public library setting. Children's services cannot evolve successfully without a blending of these conceptual frameworks. Librarians need continually to weigh what they do in relation to what they know and understand about children and families, themselves, and library service. Libraries, in fact, may be in the unique position to integrate, blend, and create the "public model" of early childhood service for young children and families.

## DEVELOPMENTALLY APPROPRIATE ENVIRONMENTS
### Selected Resources

Ammon, M. S. 1992. Literacy development: Problems and possibilities. Part II, Home influences and early literacy development. *Human Relations* 18, no. 5 (September/October): 1–5.

Anselmo, S. and W. Franz. 1995. *Early childhood development prenatal through age eight.* 2d ed. Englewood, N.J.: Prentice Hall.

Bearer, C. 1995. Environmental health hazards: How children are different from adults. *The Future of Children* 5, no. 2: 11–26.

Berk, L. and A. Winsler. 1995. *Scaffolding children's learning: Vygotsky and early childhood education.* Washington, D.C.: National Association for the Education of Young Children.

Bredekamp, S. and C. Copple, eds. 1997. *Developmentally appropriate practice in early childhood programs.* Washington, D.C.: National Association for the Education of Young Children.

Bredekamp, S., and T. Rosegrant, eds. 1992. *Reaching potentials: Appropriate curriculum and assessment for young children.* Vol. 1. Washington, D.C.: National Association for the Education of Young Children.

———. 1995. *Reaching potentials: Appropriate curriculum and assessment for young children.* Vol. 2. Washington, D.C.: National Association for the Education of Young Children.

Child Development Associates National Credentialing Program. 1986. *Infant/toddler caregivers in center-based programs.* Washington, D.C.: CDA National Credentialing Program.

Cole, E., and C. Schaefer. 1990. Can young children be art critics? *Young Children* (January): 33–38.

Feeney, S., and E. Moravcik. 1987. A thing of beauty: Aesthetic development in young children. *Young Children* 42, no. 6:6–15.

Fogel, A. 1997. *Infancy: infant, family, and society.* 3rd ed. New York: West.

Gestwicki, C. 1995. *Developmentally appropriate practice: Curriculum and development in early education.* Albany, N.Y.: Delmar.

Greenman, J. 1988. *Children's environments that work.* Redmond, Wash.: Exchange Press.

Immroth, B. F., and V. Ash-Geisler, eds. 1995. *Achieving school readiness.* Chicago: American Library Association.

Kane, D. 1985. *Environmental hazards to young children.* Phoenix, Ariz.: The Oryx Press.

Katz, L. 1987. What should young children be learning? ERIC, ED290554.

Katz, L., D. Evangelou, and J. Hartman. 1990. *The case for mixed-age grouping in early education.* Washington, D.C.: National Association for the Education of Young Children.

Kendrick, A. S., R. Kaufmann, and K. Messenger, eds. 1988. *Healthy young children: A manual for programs.* Washington, D.C.: National Association for the Education of Young Children.

Kerlavage, M. 1995. A bunch of naked ladies and a tiger: Children's responses to adult works of art. In *The visual arts and early childhood learning,* ed.

C. Thompson. Reston, Va.: The National Art Education Association, ED383643.

Kostelnik, Marjorie J. 1993. *Developmentally appropriate programs.* ERIC, ED356101.

Kuchner, J. 1996. Art and the untutored eye: Sharing the art of different cultures with young children and their families, Proceedings of the National Coalition for Campus Child Care Annual Conference (Milwaukee).

Neuman, S. B., and K. Roskos. 1990. Play, print, and purpose: Enriching play environments for literacy development. *The Reading Teacher* 44, no. 3. (November): 214–21.

Reynolds, E. 1996. *Guiding young children: A child-centered approach.* Mountain View, Calif.: Mayfield.

Spodek, B., and O. Saracho. 1994. *Right from the start: Teaching children ages three to eight.* Needham Heights, Mass.: Allyn and Bacon.

Sue, D. W., and D. Sue. 1977. Barriers to effective cross-cultural counseling. *Journal of Counseling Psychology* 24, no. 5: 420–29.

Thompson, C., ed. 1995. *The visual arts and early childhood learning.* Reston, Va.: National Art Education Association.

Trawick-Smith, J. 1997. *Early childhood development: A multicultural perspective.* Englewood Cliffs, N.J.: Prentice-Hall.

Weinstein, C., and T. David, eds. 1987. *Spaces for children: The built environment and child development.* New York: Plenum.

Zirpoli, T. 1995. *Understanding and affecting the behavior of young children.* Englewood Cliffs, N.J.: Prentice Hall.

# *2*

# Social Environment

**R**ecurring patterns of interpersonal interactions construct the social environment. People enter a physical setting with a set of expectations about the particular institution. Prominent among these expectations are ideas about the ability of the setting to meet their needs and beliefs about how others will behave and react.

Interpersonal interactions are influenced by the relationships that develop over time and the social or professional networks that evolve within a community. When adults and children become regular users of library services and programs, they begin to recognize librarians and staff and to build a sense of shared experiences. Although current interests, abilities, temperament, past histories, and developmental stage contribute to the nature of these interpersonal connections, the degree to which these budding relationships are nurtured influence a family's feelings about the library.

The social environment has an impact in all areas of the library but its importance is magnified in the children's area. This is the place where first impressions of libraries are formed. Families new to the community, adults new to their roles as parents, and all children are especially sensitive to messages of acceptance and welcome.

## MESSAGES OF WELCOME

Both the physical and the social environment should provide messages of welcome. Signs, pictures, symbols, furniture and equipment, displays, and collections can indicate that a place is set aside for the special use of young children and their families. These examples of welcome messages are embedded in the physical environment. Chapter 3 describes the physical environment in detail.

Being greeted upon arrival is one of the first verbal messages of welcome and respect. The style of communication creates a social climate that is a significant aspect of the library experience. It is especially important for librarians to notice children, greet them, and interact with them, as well as greet the parents, caregivers, or older family members who accompany them. Throughout the community, young children are frequently ignored or literally overlooked. Yet both children and adults appreciate being recognized by name. Within the general North American culture, eye contact and friendly verbal forms of address are used to convey interest, attention, welcome, and acceptance.

# Cultural Variations in Verbal and Nonverbal Communication

A great deal of communication is based on body language, facial expressions, and the use of personal space. The predominance and style of these communicative pathways vary among cultures, as do content and pattern of verbal communication. Although the European-American paradigm is to make eye contact with children and to expect eye contact from children as a sign of alert attentiveness and respect, this is not universal. Among some Native American cultures, direct eye contact from a parent is used as a way of reprimanding or punishing children (Sue and Sue 1977). In many African-American, Puerto Rican, Mexican-American (Trawick-Smith 1997), and Japanese families (Sue and Sue 1977), children learn to keep their gaze down and away from the adult's face as a sign of respect.

Children learn to use and interpret culturally specific rules for displaying emotions. Although smiling is most frequently associated with positive regard, it may also be used to cover embarrassment. In cultures that emphasize the maintenance of harmonious relations even in the face of genuine conflict of ideas, a smile may be used to avoid displays of anger or sadness. This type of emotional control is valued within Korean (Farver and Shin 1997), Japanese, and Chinese (Kuchner 1984) cultural communities.

Comfortable speaking distance and amount of acceptable interpersonal touching are other components of communication with cross-cultural variability. Within Hispanic-American communities, greetings between friends and acquaintances are frequently accompanied by some form of casual touching or bodily contact (Sue and Sue 1977). This type of physical contact may make individuals from other backgrounds uncomfortable.

European-Americans tend to be viewed by members of some cultures as overly talkative. Other cultural communities view silence as a positive form of communication. Silence may be used for emphasis, as an indication of respect, or to establish and maintain harmonious relationships. Individuals from European-American backgrounds often interpret silence as an invitation to speak or as an interruption in communication that needs to be filled. Overlapping speech, on the other hand, may be viewed as a sign of immaturity. This is not the perspective within cultures that view people talking over each other's verbalizations as a sign of enthusiasm and involvement in the subject matter

(Trawick-Smith 1997). There are also variations in the acceptability of children addressing adults, especially asking questions, or questioning an adult's behavior.

Communities that libraries serve change over time, as does an individual's identification within a culture. Librarians should begin with the communication style that is most comfortable for them while being prepared to make appropriate adjustments to a style that synchronizes with the people they serve. Being aware of and sensitive to the predominant cultures within the community are part of a librarian's professional responsibility.

## Interactions among Staff

The social environment is shaped by many levels of communication: the interactions between librarians and patrons, the interactions among staff members, and the type of interactions that are encouraged among children, parents, caregivers, and early childhood professionals within the library. When staff members treat each other with courtesy and respect, this sets the tone for other social exchanges. Librarians who are aware of the ongoing pattern of interaction within the library and who are ready to assist patrons and other staff members as needed are able to generate a communal feeling of support.

Maintaining confidentiality in the area of personal relationships among staff and between the librarian and patron adds to the overall feeling of respect. This includes restricting conversations about a child's behavior so that only the people involved are privy to the concern.

## CREATING ENVIRONMENTS THAT NURTURE LEARNING

There are many micro-environments within the library that have their own physical boundaries, social structure, and expectations. In any particular library, these may include the children's reference desk, the circulation desk, the audiovisual center, a computer area, the early childhood collections section, a museum or special display area, manipulative and play areas, as well as rooms for particular programs and workshops. Children need to know what is expected of them in each of these areas. A critical role of the librarian is to make sure that these expectations are within the child's abilities. For example, young children should not be expected to keep quiet or remain in one place for long periods of time.

Librarians need to be sensitive to the different demands of the environment(s) and be willing and available to assist both adults and children with specific relevant issues, concerns, or questions. Recognizing both the child and the adult as worthy of individualized attention is an important aspect of a responsive early childhood program. Staff within these settings need the education and training that will enable them to respond appropriately to young children, school-age children, and adults.

## Acknowledging the Individual

Creating ways to make both children and their parents and caregivers feel successful and important is the library staff's responsibility. Using specific descriptive phrases to point out positive aspects of the child's ongoing behavior is more satisfying to the child than using broad praise with little informational content. Attending to behavior and skill acquisition rather than to personal characteristics is one way to avoid making value judgments. This strategy provides a safeguard against using language laden with stereotypes.

Narrating a description of an ongoing activity is a strategy that positively acknowledges the child and encourages emerging language. It provides the child with a model of language structure and vocabulary that matches the focus of the child's action.

Sincerity and genuine appreciation of a child's growing competence are central to communicating affirmations. When children are in the process of learning something new, they are literally and figuratively stepping into unknown territory. This involves taking a risk, a risk of failure. When children receive recognition for their mastery attempts, they are willing to continue trying. Making errors and self-correcting are a part of learning. Children who find that their exploration of new experiences and skills repeatedly leads to criticism are less open to learning new concepts and strategies.

## Scaffolding: Supporting Autonomy and Nurturing Learning

Children want to do things by themselves yet may need assistance. Library staff must be skilled at balancing levels of involvement and intrusion. Children continue to challenge themselves when a responsive and receptive adult is present. "Scaffolding" provides the best physical, cognitive, and emotional support.

Offering a stepstool to allow a child to reach a book from a high shelf or holding a paper flat so that a child will have an easier time writing are examples of scaffolding or supporting without eliminating autonomy. Children function independently when they feel independent. Adjusting the amount of information offered in answering a reference question to match a child's abilities or helping a child divide a task into manageable segments are other examples of scaffolding. Asking clarifying questions, pointing out relationships, or encouraging children to make predictions about future events based on current behaviors will create scaffolds for the acquisition of new knowledge and understanding. Scaffolds for enhancing intrapersonal understanding occur when adults help children express feelings. Interpersonal learning occurs when adults help children use words to negotiate.

# Active Listening

Active listening is a critical skill for working with both young children and adults. Active listening begins with being available and approachable. One way that adults communicate their availability and openness to a child is by making a point of sitting, kneeling, or bending until they are at a child's eye level. This is not the same as bending over the child. The former invites communication. The latter position, which suggests being overpowered, can be intimidating. Making eye contact, smiling, and taking the time to allow an adult, alone or with children, to approach and begin a conversation or ask a question also invites communication from parents or caregivers.

Active listening focuses not only on the words and nonverbal messages but also on the feeling, tone, or emotional content of the message. The listener needs to empathize with the emotional quality of the message as well as with the content. After absorbing the apparent information, the next step is for the listener to reflect back the ideas and feelings presented. Reflection as a step in active listening communicates comprehension, verifies interpretations, corrects misunderstandings, and fine-tunes the expressed meaning. The emotional content of a message may be an important cue in determining which resources best match the patron's interest or request.

Sometimes, it may be necessary to restate a young child's questions or provide an expanded version. Expansions add selected words to the child's utterance, using the immediate shared context to provide information about meaning. The response both acknowledges understanding and provides a model of correct language use. Establishing shared referents is an important step in communication and in language acquisition. Once the librarian is focused on the child's interest, additional comments can to used to extend a discussion.

A calm, warm, and reassuring tone of voice is also important when working with parents or caregivers. Brusque, harsh, strident, or impatient tones of voice can change the meaning even when the words provide useful information. It is frequently the tone of voice that leads adults to decide that a librarian is uninterested in their concerns or is passing judgment on the content of their request. Even young children learn to extract meaning from tone of voice before they understand the meaning of words.

Librarians must direct social interactions to the parent or caregiver as well as to the child. Parents are often the main link to resource and information access for young children. Frequently, it is the parent who asks the librarian for help on behalf of the child. Active listening is required in order to match the collections, services, or programs effectively with the stated or implied needs and interests of either child or adult. When working with an adult and young child simultaneously, the librarian may need to untangle whether the request is driven by the adult's need or appears to be appropriate to the child's interests and abilities. Different recommendations or suggestions would flow from each of these assessments.

This information triad of child, parent, and librarian requires an understanding of child development, an appreciation of family systems, and a recognition of the parent as an adult learner. Ideally, engaging both the parent and child in the information exchange process is requisite to the provision of quality library service for young children. It underscores the librarian's role as mentor in the lifelong learning process. Chapter 4 provides an in-depth look at aspects of parent participation in library-based early childhood services.

# PROVIDING GUIDELINES FOR BEHAVIOR AND SETTING LIMITS

Library policies concerning running, climbing, eating and drinking, and adult supervision of children should be available for patrons and posted visibly in the early childhood area. Ideally, young children in public libraries should be supervised by a family member or caregiver. Librarians may have to step into situations to ensure safety and to establish realistic and consistent limits on behavior.

Monitoring the ongoing activity from strategic vantage points throughout the room makes librarians more approachable and helps them intervene before a conflict or potentially dangerous situation arises. Developing the ability to focus on individual children and also scan the entire room is essential. Other positive guidance techniques include altering the physical environment, modeling appropriate behavior, scaffolding, setting limits, providing choices, and redirecting.

## Setting Limits

Setting limits is different from enforcing rules. Rules are arbitrary and often involve placing restrictions on everyone and every circumstance without the flexibility to adapt to unique individual situations. Focusing attention on rule enforcement invites people to challenge or attempt to circumvent the rules. Limits reflect the changing context of the social and physical setting while paying attention to boundaries of safety, respect for the rights of others, and individual responsibility for behavior.

Setting, acknowledging, and explaining limits help children develop self-control. Requests for changes in behavior should always assume that the individual has the ability to change and will take appropriate action. Stated in their positive form, requests point to the desired behavior rather than the cessation of the inappropriate action. Children learn active problem-solving skills when adults engage in limit setting.

Young children need to learn the rules of public places such as libraries. The library's expectations of appropriate behavior may be different from those at home or in the child-care setting. Informing while using a congenial tone of voice is an effective way of setting limits. For example, "Bookshelves are made for holding books, not people. You may wish to use a stool to help you reach the book or sit on a pillow while you are reading." The child can then select other places to sit or climb. The responsibility for solving the problem involves the child, not just the rules of the institution. The child identifies an appropriate or satisfactory alternative to current behavior and chooses to substitute a safe activity for one that is dangerous or potentially damaging.

Sometimes "I-messages" are used to indicate the reason for the limits. "I worry that you will get hurt if you continue to climb on the bookshelves because they are not made for climbing and could easily fall over." This expresses the adult's feeling, the action that is occurring, and the reason for the desired change. The child is not labeled as bad, disobedient, stupid, or untrustworthy, and a supportive atmosphere and flexible environment are created.

Young children occasionally have difficulty inhibiting an action in progress and need gentle physical guidance toward acceptable places and actions. Easily recognizable human physical barriers such as an outstretched arm reaching behind a group of young children or a light touch on a shoulder can keep them moving in a desired direction.

# Offering Choices

An important part of any early childhood setting is offering appropriate choices. Children become more interested and engaged with their environment when guided and encouraged to make real choices based on their individual needs. Selecting books, toys, construction materials, and activities allows young children to initiate their own play and provides them with positive learning experiences.

# Redirecting

Redirection is a useful tool for positive change. It offers an alternative object or activity to a child who attempts a dangerous goal or tries to take an object from another child. In this instance, having multiple copies of toys and books available minimizes conflict and encourages parallel play. Parallel play occurs when two or more children sitting near each other play with similar toys or objects without exchanging words or objects. Parallel play generally evolves to more socially interactive play as children mature.

# PLANNING PROGRAMS AND ACTIVITIES

Program content and design emerge from the knowledge of how children learn as well as what they need to know. Learning is playful, interactive, multidimensional, and interdisciplinary. Planning considers all of these facets and is a critical part of early childhood library services.

## The Framework: Balance and Structure

Each individual session with young children should be built around a clear structure and feature a playful approach to activities. Play provides the intrinsic motivation for focused attention and cooperative social interactions. Depending on the age of the children, programs vary in pace, intensity, and social organization. Each program should strike a balance between staff-directed and child-initiated segments, individual and group organization, and active and sedentary activities. Integrating toys and interactive materials in combination with picture books enhances programs and involves the children in the learning process. Librarians need to be flexible, willing to be responsive to the children's cues and interests.

Programs and workshops should facilitate an experimental approach to individual discovery that recognizes children's simultaneous involvement in several types of learning. Lilian Katz's (1987) description of the acquisition of skills, facts, emotions, and dispositions provides a guideline for understanding the many layers of learning that occur. In the course of a library program, children may have the opportunity to practice discrete skills such as cutting or counting. They may acquire information or knowledge about particular events or take part in experiences that will assist them in concept formation. At the same time, they are receiving messages that will influence their feelings of competence and confidence in the pursuit of these goals. The adult who acts as the guide is positioned to encourage the children to want to discover more on their own. Developing a disposition toward wanting to explore new ideas and an intrinsic feeling of satisfaction from the process of learning may be the most important lessons for setting children on the road to lifelong learning.

## Staffing

Well-organized staffing is an important variable in the quality of a program. Research strongly suggests that the higher the ratio of staff to children, the more positive are the outcomes, including less aggression and greater cooperation among children. A sufficiently staffed program promotes the physical, social, emotional, and cognitive development of children.

Ideally, there should be two adults in addition to parents or caregivers available for each group, with a librarian or professional and a paraprofessional sharing responsibility. Though few libraries have the staff or volunteer numbers to accomplish this goal, it is important to recognize this standard and work toward accomplishing it.

Scheduling the same staff member in an ongoing program is essential. A child gains a sense of comfort and security with a familiar program presenter and the rituals and the patterns of a particular program. Librarians attuned to the needs of young children will help children feel more comfortable and secure in the library environment.

## Audience

The younger the children, the greater the need for a small group and a low adult-child ratio. The recommended group size for infants is six to eight with one parent or caregiver per child; for toddlers, ten to twelve with at least one parent or caregiver for every two children; for three- and four-year-olds, fifteen to eighteen with optional parent or caregiver participation; and for children between the ages of five and eight, eighteen to twenty-two with optional parent or caregiver participation.

Parent-child workshops set up as early learning centers and early childhood drop-in activity areas can accommodate larger groups depending on the actual size of the space and the resources available. These services do not require an organized group activity or staff leadership but focus on the interaction between the parent and the child.

## Mixed Age Groupings

Young children may acquire skills more rapidly in some domains than in others. For example, one child may be highly verbal but awkward in fine motor coordination while another may attend to letters and numbers while having difficulties with emotional control. This variation is important to note when making program decisions.

In mixed age groups, older children can function as "master players" incorporating younger children into episodes of more complex play than the younger ones could reach on their own. Groups of this nature can provide opportunities for the older children to assume responsibility and practice cooperative leadership.

Simply putting children of different ages together, however, is no guarantee of successful outcomes. Factors such as group size, age range, proportion of older to younger children, and the expectations of the program's structure and activities strongly influence the success of mixed age groupings. Using the developmental guidelines for the age of the youngest children is a strategy to determine optimal group size.

## Program Period

The length of a program period should be based on the age of the children, the ratio of adults to children, and the variety of planned activities. Basic guidelines acknowledge that the younger the child, the shorter the programming time; the greater the need for parent/caregiver involvement; the greater the need for individualizing; the shorter the time devoted to group activity; and the more lively and action-oriented the program content.

For example, a twenty-minute time span is sufficient for an infant and toddler story time. Thirty minutes is appropriate for preschool children, while primary grade children can manage thirty to sixty minutes. When conducting a parent-child workshop with toddlers, however, an hour and a quarter seems to work best. In this type of program, parents and children work individually with many different materials. No organized group activity takes place until "circle time" closes the session. Late arrival, early departure, or absence from circle time can be accommodated without affecting the program.

When young children and their parents or caregivers visit the library on a drop-in basis, the same ground rules can apply. The amount of time children spend on activities varies based on the child's individual behavior or attention span and the parent's resourcefulness and time constraints as well as the amount of materials and space available.

## Room Arrangement

The nature of the social grouping will influence seating patterns. Children who regularly attend programs together or who come with a class or child-care group will have established friendship patterns that may govern individual seating choices. Sufficient seating locations need to be provided for all children.

The physical arrangement of the early childhood area and the program setting is critical. When the program format requires children to face a presenter, they should be close enough to establish visual contact. Parents should be given an opportunity to observe or participate. Younger children may prefer that their parent remain physically close. Setting up the same room arrangement for each program in a series provides children with a sense of security and comfort. Chapter 3 provides further ideas about the impact of the physical environment.

## PROGRAM CONTENT

All programs for young children should include some type of investigation or interaction with concrete objects. Young children learn best when they have the opportunity to use all of their senses. They are in the process of constructing their understanding of the world. Even three- to five-year-olds are more likely to understand relationships, concepts, and problem-solving strategies when they have had the opportunity of using objects or investigating them firsthand. Concrete, meaningful experiences are the basis for early learning. It is important for a librarian to incorporate these experiences into programs that feature books along with auditory and visual media.

There is a predictable cycle of learning for all ages. Becoming aware that something exists—whether the something is an object, a person, a relationship, an event, or a symbol—precedes all other learning. Creating a print-rich environment for children supports the first step in literacy: print awareness. This immersion in written language that has real usefulness in identifying things, communicating wishes, and reaching goals parallels the naturally occurring involvement with oral language.

Interest in and curiosity about books also begin with awareness. Using and handling books, as in turning pages, and expecting to hear words or narratives in conjunction with particular pages in a book are actions to be experimented with, practiced, and applied to related situations. The language and event patterns in traditional tales and well-written contemporary stories for young children help them to learn about story structure. They become familiar with different settings, themes, plots, and resolutions that enable them to make accurate predictions and to apply this awareness to extract meaning from more complex writings. Through songs, word games, and repeated stories children learn about narrative order: beginning, middle, and end. They are also learning about word use and meaning, rhymes and rhyming patterns.

Infants are introduced to these language sequences through playful, supportive interactions with adults. Programs for infants and parents provide models of interactive social play. Although songs, rhymes, and playful behavior sequences are frequently passed down from generation to generation or "picked up" informally, there are still many new parents who have not had the opportunity to hear them used or have not yet begun to appreciate the importance of these one-on-one playful interactions.

Books introduce children to new ideas. To understand something fully, it is also necessary to explore it. Children learn best when they act on objects and interact with people. Thinking about the consequences of action leads to new knowledge. Therefore, it is important to link information from books with real world experiences in each program or session.

Developmentally appropriate skill building is essential to the quality of programs. Programming activities and materials for preschool children should be embedded in opportunities to build skills and concepts through meaningful hands-on experiences. Children need multiple concrete experiences to construct an understanding of the words that they hear. The reading experience can extend in many directions including science, mathematics, art, and interpersonal relations.

Careful observations are the foundations of science. Young children are careful observers. They begin to group observations and make predictions about future events. Well-developed programs encourage children to observe, describe, and begin to group or classify physical phenomena. The process of carefully describing events strengthens communication skills and aids in vocabulary development.

Mathematically oriented experiences also have a place in library programs. Introducing young children to the language of quantities, sizes, and shapes and connecting these terms with concrete experience provide a foundation for learning other mathematical concepts. Concepts such as one-to-one correspondence, big and little, or even the idea of subtraction or "take away" can be explored using senses such as touch and movement.

An introduction to the visual arts occurs as young children examine the illustrations in books. Reproductions of works of art and examples of contemporary art stimulate discussion and interaction. Beautiful illustrations increase children's attraction to books and introduce them to the vocabulary of line, shape, and color. Young children begin to develop visual literacy when they express their own interpretation of the art that they see.

Children enjoy creating art. They talk about their creations as they evolve. Although it pleases children to take an item home or to have it displayed in the library, quality art experiences for young children should not be product driven. The process of creating the art is more important than what it looks like at the end of a session.

Centering a story time program on a familiar theme or a basic emotion helps young children relate new ideas and materials to their own personal experiences and relationships. Librarians can assist children in analyzing new concepts and skills and help them compare new experiences to those that are familiar. Children have an inherent motivation to become competent and to increase their understanding. This is coupled with a desire to practice newly acquired mental abilities. Activities to foster physical and motor coordination are also a part of an effective program.

Diversity is an essential consideration in book and material selection. One cannot assume that all program participants will have the same complement of family members or celebrate the same seasonal and religious holidays. Books and stories should be selected so that programs feature materials grounded in different traditions. Stories should illustrate a range of abilities and family patterns. It is important to keep in mind that the home-based experiences and family configurations of today's young children vary greatly.

Caution should be exercised in selecting stories of divorce, death, and even pregnancy for a general audience. These are topics that are more suitable for intimate sharing or in settings where the topic is known to be relevant to the particular child's life experience. Children may not understand some of these challenging issues and find the topics anxiety provoking.

Humor, on the other hand, is a rich resource. Young children appreciate humor based on exaggeration, opposites, or mislabeling.

They enjoy situations that make adults in general appear misguided. Shared laughter can create a sense of group cohesion.

All children need a visual focus during story time. They need to sit close enough to see the pictures and share in an open discussion about the events in the story. Librarians encourage conversation by asking open-ended questions about interesting story events and illustrations. Questions can be used to elicit higher-order thinking skills such as comparing, recognizing patterns, interpreting, making connections, and transferring knowledge. Although simple recall questions can begin the process, they should not be the only type of interaction. Reading a story out loud is also an opportunity to add emotional or comic coloration to characters, to use appropriately varied tones of voice to distinguish character and mood, and to demonstrate enthusiasm and pleasure in reading.

## TRANSITIONS: AN OPPORTUNITY FOR LEARNING

Transition times often highlight the most basic social learning that occurs in libraries. Every program contains a range of transition points, transitions into the program from the children's area, transitions between group and individual activity, and transitions from the program to the world beyond the library.

Even simple transitions can be a source of stress for a young child. The juxtaposition of two things that are desirable, such as staying with a parent or participating in a program, may be overwhelming. For another child the difficult transition may be leaving an enjoyable activity. Children need to have time to complete interesting activities that they have started so that they leave the program with a sense of accomplishment.

Creating predictable rituals or activity sequences at the beginning and the end of a program can help children feel successful in their ability to predict events. Building time for these transitional activities within the program, including time to say good-bye to toys and peers as well as time for the librarian to talk with individual parents or caregivers and their children, is critical.

The ability to adapt to new situations, settings, programs, and routines is a component of temperament. Some children need more warning about change in activity. Other children are particularly sensitive to new social situations, waiting and watching on the sidelines until they feel ready to participate. These children have often been described as "slow to warm up."

Many young children need to know that their parent is close at hand in a public place. Cultural and individual differences influence young children's comfort level when listening, talking, or playing at a distance from their parents and significant caregivers. Daily variations in a child's need to be within touching, viewing, or hearing distance of a parent also occur. Variations are influenced by fatigue, noise level, numbers and ages of children, and the nature of the activities. Even older preschool and primary grade children need parents to remain in the library and be available. Sometimes an older child may be hesitant to interact with the librarian or may need the parent during a program. While some children remain on the sidelines throughout a program, many can gradually be drawn into the activity.

Opening programs with a song, a rhyme, or a familiar puppet has long been part of story time. The ritual provides a signal for children that certain events will occur and that certain behaviors are expected. It provides boundary definition to the setting. Children enjoy repeating favorite songs and fingerplays as part of program rituals. Learning predictable word sequences and word-action combinations assists the emergence of literacy.

Knowing children's names maintains a smooth flow in any interaction. Identifying or creating name tags is an activity to transition children into a program. In multi-session programs, a symbol alongside a name makes it easier for the youngest children to recognize their name tag at subsequent meetings. Asking children to choose their own symbol and to select their own name tag helps them become aware of symbols and letters. Wearing a name tag makes a child feel noticed and important.

Parents may find name tags useful in helping both their children and themselves meet friends. Parent participants in programs appreciate the use of adult name tags to help them learn the names of others in the community with children the same age as their own. Adult friendships are often facilitated by activities initially directed toward their children. Parents who do not participate in the program may also be comforted that they can be located by the staff, if needed, when their child is wearing a name tag.

Creating library patrons who are lifelong learners is a major goal of programming. Program participation stimulates interest in materials among children and parents. Multiple copies of books used in programs, handouts with the words of the nursery rhymes or songs sung as part of a program, and bibliographies of related materials are necessary "tools of the trade" when working with young children and their families. Displaying related books and materials expands ideas presented in the program. When preparing programs for young children, it is often helpful to have these selected items for circulation readily available in the programming room. This accommodates the tired child, assists in the transition from the library to home, and guides parents in appropriate materials to use at home.

## SOCIAL AND EMOTIONAL LEARNING

Social interaction is an inherent part of the learning process. Young children learn different things from interacting with adults than they do from exchanges with children similar in abilities and interests. Taking the responsibility for guiding or helping younger children offers another type of social learning.

The ability to understand other people and to work cooperatively involves a number of complex social skills that fall in the domain of emotional intelligence. Being able to understand the feelings of others requires the ability to see a situation from the perspective of another person and then to empathize with that view. Taking on different roles in play is one way in which to practice this emergent mental ability. The ability to wait or postpone immediate gratification and to regulate one's own emotions are equally important aspects of the social curriculum that will influence subsequent success.

Social knowledge includes being able to identify and understand social symbols, rituals, myths, and values. Young children do not automatically recognize and conform to social conventions. When a child is told to smile and say thank you for a gift that is not liked, the child is learning about social conventions.

## Validating Emotions

In the library setting, the role of the staff or parent is to validate emotions and help the child find the right words to express feelings. This is a first step for the child in learning to find appropriate outlets for strong emotions, as well as resolutions to everyday sources of interpersonal conflict.

Since anger in young children is most often expressed physically, it is beneficial to young children to help them find acceptable outlets through physical action. A young child who repeatedly throws objects or hits is better able to manage the library experience if allowed to run around outside beforehand. At home or in a regular child-care setting, kicking a ball or punching a pillow or play dough or banging on a toy drum may offer relief. Identifying an emotion can be followed by goal-directed problem solving or negotiations that model alternative methods for reaching a successful conclusion.

Strategies for interacting with children and adults are also teaching techniques. An expanded description of teaching behaviors is outlined in chapter 7. These widely recognized teaching methods need to be incorporated into the librarian's array of skills.

## ASSESSMENT OF SOCIAL ENVIRONMENT

The social environment is influenced by all facets of the children's department including the librarian's work with parents and her or his own level of education and training. Acquiring knowledge of child development and instilling this knowledge into practice, listening and becoming sensitive to parents and their role in the learning process, and implementing emotionally appropriate programs are at the center of a socially appropriate environment. Chapter 1 provides a listing of resources that further assist librarians in developing and evaluating appropriate learning environments for young children (see pp. 12–13).

A picture of the library's current social environment, acknowledgment of the individual librarian's ability and responsibility to understand appropriate behavior and developmental milestones, and a willingness to change are necessary in order to move toward "better practice." Assessment of the social environment occurs within the context of everyday experiences.

Direct observations and interviews, running records, and checklists, described in Part Two, are readily available strategies for gathering and recording information about ongoing practices. A parent focus group is another vehicle that often garners information regarding a library's social environment for children and parents. Specific tools for assessing the social environment include forms B-1, B-2, B-4, B-12, C-1, C-2, C-3, C-4, C-5, and D-4.

REFERENCES

Farver, J., and Y. Shin. 1997. Social pretend play in Korean and Anglo-American preschoolers. *Child Development* 68, no. 3: 544–56.

Katz, L. 1987. What should young children be learning? ERIC, ED290554.

Kuchner, J. 1984. Chinese-American and European-American mothers and infants: Cultural influences in the first three months of life. ERIC, ED308985.

Sue, D. W., and D. Sue. 1977. Barriers to effective cross-cultural counseling. *Journal of Counseling Psychology* 24, no. 5: 420–29.

Trawick-Smith, J. 1997. *Early childhood development: A multicultural perspective*. Englewood Cliffs, N.J.: Prentice-Hall.

# 3

# Physical Environment

The physical and emotional health and safety of young children and their families should be paramount in the design and maintenance of the library's physical environment. Although young children spend the majority of their time in the children's section, they often accompany adult patrons using the full range of library spaces. Children's librarians must have an eye on ensuring the safety and acceptance of its youngest patrons throughout the entire library.

Most libraries regularly evaluate the amount, arrangement, and use of available space. Throughout this process, it is important to understand that the physical environment affects the behavior and development of both children and adults. The quality of the physical space, equipment, and materials influences the level of involvement of children and the caliber of the interaction among children, their parents and caregivers, librarians and other library staff.

The physical environment of the children's area invites young children and their families to become involved in active learning. By offering children and adults access to a wide range of age-appropriate materials and providing a place for families to meet comfortably and share their experiences, the library is furthering its mission. Its physical environment sets the stage for the development of friendships and the expansion of social and professional networks. The multiple serendipitous and planned interactions that take place are part of the fabric of community life.

The physical environment alone cannot create a climate of responsiveness to individual young children and their families. The arrangement of both fixed and flexible features and the nature and ease of access to materials and resources are integral aspects of the environment. Space allocation, design, and the availability of materials convey messages of acceptance or rejection of individual interests and values, strengths and capabilities, ethnicity, gender, and life style.

The physical environment communicates to each child and adult encoded messages about expected behaviors and actions, the people who regularly use a setting, the type of formal and informal social structure, and the emotional climate that is encouraged. Environments for young children must be physically safe, socially enhancing, emotionally nurturing, and intellectually and aesthetically stimulating. Design should prevent accidental injuries and discourage the spread of disease.

Decisions that are made about fixed features like walls, floors, and ceilings, and semi-fixed features such as furnishings and equipment influence the ease of communication, the potential for independent choices, the nature of social groupings, and the participants' feelings of comfort and competence. Pathways and lines of sight also have a direct bearing on the supervision of activities.

# EARLY CHILDHOOD AREA

Size, scale, and access dominate the discussion of the physical environment both from the perspective of safety and from the way the features communicate encouragement and welcome. These features are especially important when creating spaces and services for young children and their families. Families are composed of individuals who vary greatly in ease of mobility, degree of independence, and problem-solving skills including the ability to ask for assistance. The extent to which young children and their caregivers move through a space with ease and access the materials and services available determines the degree to which they feel that they belong. It will influence their frequency of library use and, in turn, their sense of ownership.

The size of the rooms and facilities allotted to young children and their location within the building provide insight to the role these services play within the institution. The distance from the entrance and the nature of the obstacles presented will encourage or discourage use of the children's area. Parents and caregivers hold onto or carry young children. Frequently, they are managing carriages or strollers and carrying books and library materials. Stairways, long hallways or large items of furniture, bookshelves, desks, or other equipment that block passageways to the children's section are all barriers.

# Space Organization and Room Management

Young children are just beginning to learn the rules of behavior that govern public and private places. From the perspective of a young child, each setting has its own action potential. Young children do not as yet have the cognitive ability to create a single rule from multiple individual experiences. Transferring behavior from home, child-care centers, school, or playground may not provide children with the specific information relevant to behavior in libraries. Librarians encourage children to approach the library setting with a sense of comfort and emotional security by filling the area with images and equipment scaled to their height, adapted to their motor abilities, and directed toward their interests and style of learning.

Platforms, pits, and partial walls can be used to define an activity area. Tiered level areas 3 to 6 inches high and 12 inches deep can offer surfaces for multiple functions (Olds 1987). While these architectural details may unintentionally create obstacles to participation, they often provide choice surfaces for propping books, balancing puzzles, manipulating small toys, practicing repetitive motor behaviors, and engaging in pretend play.

During the field study (*Early Childhood Quality Review* 1995), one reviewer noted: "Two children who had recently met at the library were expanding their relationship through shared pretend. They were observed using the upper levels of the built-in story hour pit as the dock/boat area to find protection from the sharks and other sea monsters who were currently inhabiting the depths of this library's story hour pit, two steps below."

Collective pretend is also promoted through the creation of key walk-in thematic places such as boats, trains, or houses whose natural features can be used as private retreats, for parent-child reading or for small group activities. Young children learn with their whole body. The exploration and use of a wide variety of physical spaces provide concrete experiences upon which to build abstract concepts. The "book barge" (a boat-shaped seating area) of one field site library became a place for learning about over and under for two brothers both less than three years of age. The older child alternately led the way over and under the seats and rails, challenging his younger sibling to follow (1995).

Physical places afford different types of behaviors.* Physical objects, places, spaces, and structures have a range of affordances that may differ according to one's perspective and abilities. For the young child, the affordance of a place is influenced by its height, scale, arrangements of openings, and moveable parts as well as the child's development of gross and fine motor coordination. Young children do not consider a place or object according to usual or stereotypical definitions of use. From the perspective of a young child, steps and edges invite both sitting and climbing. Surfaces ask to be stretched out upon, stood upon, or provide handholds for hoisting efforts that allow the young child to view people and interactions otherwise hidden from view. Lower flat surfaces are good resting places for books or objects. Shapes that extend from a fixed structure are perceived by children as levers or hangers.

Anything that can be moved, turned, poked, or manipulated will be. On one visit to a field site library a child, whose mother was busy at the reference desk, approached a bench with a side shaped like a rabbit. The toddler was fascinated by the elongated ears which he proceeded to move up and down. From there he proceeded to the child-height globe, spinning it with gusto (1995).

---

*The *affordance* of a place or object refers to the kinds of operations and manipulations that can be done to it.

For safety reasons, heating units and electrical sockets need to be covered or out of reach and all surfaces need to be maintained free of splinters, protruding nails, broken or loose parts, and sharp edges. Furniture should have rounded corners or protectors.

Research investigating alternative room arrangements in child-care centers shows that rooms in which space is organized into a variety of large and small areas with clear architectural and visible differences encourage young children to make choices that evolve into complex small-group social interactions and fantasy play. Open room plans that do not differentiate activity areas or provide semi-enclosed or partial stimulus screens for spatial organization are generally noisier and require more intervention by adults to redirect random activity by children and control noise levels (Moore 1987). In this open type of environment, young children spend more time in transition between activities than in focused involvement with materials and resources.

In libraries, activity and learning centers that are easily recognizable and in which materials with similar use or themes are grouped together assist young children in extending exploration and play. Physical arrangements should allow young children to maintain their naturally occurring preferences for play in small groups of children, two to, at most, five children in a cluster. To facilitate cognitively oriented activities, each defined area should provide space for children and adults to stand, sit, and work together. Seating that allows for side-by-side options is more conducive to cooperative activities. Young children often enjoy using the floor itself as a work area. Carpet areas or clearly demarcated sections encourage this type of use. Corners or nooks with rugs, pillows, or other soft features and materials lend themselves to interpersonal sharing and play. Comfortable space for one or two children and/or an adult encourages such exchanges.

Adult-size chairs within the young children's area are more comfortable for some parents and caregivers as well as for breast-feeding mothers who may want to nurse infants while still remaining available to supervise and respond to older siblings.

## Creative Spaces and Places

The height and size of a room may be overwhelming to a young child. Children appreciate small intimate spaces. Furniture that is scaled to the size of an average three- or four-year-old, nooks, crannies, and partial enclosures can define a young children's area within a larger room. Young children generally avoid totally enclosed areas but a space surrounded on two or three sides invites entry, creates a stimulus shelter, and offers a place for solitary retreat.

Children use partially enclosed spaces or overlooks to escape from intrusive behavior or excessive social stimulation and noise, to observe group activities, to review past experiences, and to plan future actions. These are safe locations for flights of imagination and for play. The availability of private places assists children in learning to control emotions. When such physical options are not available, young children create their own defensible spaces through the arrangement of toys or furniture. Young children benefit from the voluntary control of private retreats to experience calm and escape from stimulus overload.

A number of design strategies can be used to create areas of apparent privacy or to define activity areas without obstructing visual and physical access by adults. Transparent display cases or fish tanks and open window frames, giant dollhouses, large play vehicles, or platform stages provide the illusion of privacy for young children. Latticework, rails or fencing, and variously shaped windows or portholes can serve similar purposes. While large openings need to be sufficiently large for children to climb through, railings should be properly sized to prevent infant or toddler heads from becoming stuck in the openings. According to U.S. government safety standards for infant cribs, openings of no more than $2\,^3/_8$ inches can be used.

Young children need the opportunity for making their own choices about materials and activities. A portion of the collection including books, materials, and manipulative toys should be accessible without adult assistance through an arrangement of low shelves, open bins without lids or covers, and safe, low hooks or hangers. Stable shelves strong enough to support the additional weight of a curious toddler are necessary. Each activity center should contain things that can be touched or manipulated to hold the interest of young children.

Activity areas should provide room for young children to move among the storage areas and furniture, practicing both independence and the coordination of large motor activities. Pathways carry messages about relationships between activities and convey information about expected behavior and use. Lines of movement should be free of obstructions and clearly defined for the young child. Wheelchair accessibility for both adults and children is a significant consideration. The intersection of paths provides the opportunity for children to exercise choices and make decisions. Dead ends or cul-de-sacs should be avoided. For safety reasons, alternative modes of entry into and exit from an area or center are always preferable to a single point of access and exit.

# Welcoming Infants

Infants under one year old are an integral part of a young family and are considered in the planning of family centered environments. Spaces designed primarily for use by toddlers and other young children include places for infants. Modular or portable infant areas surrounded on all sides by a solid, padded, raised barrier can be set up on a temporary basis. This allows parents to safely place pre-crawlers in a stimulating area within their sight. It prevents an infant's access to materials with small parts that can be easily ingested. Materials with small parts, suitable for five- to eight-year-olds, must be stored out of reach of infants and toddlers. Floor space or storage space needs to include rooms for strollers and carriages, and other equipment as necessary.

# CHILDREN'S ROOM

Young children learn from imitating adult behavior. Participation in adult focused interactions, even as an observer, assists young children in learning the cultural scripts for appropriate interaction. Solid boundaries and platforms or desks with tops above the heads of young children frequently interfere with this learning process. Children then use these surfaces for hanging or climbing in order to take part in the interaction. Lowering a portion of the reference desk to a height of 29 or 30 inches allows young children to see over the top of a raised surface into the adult arena. This type of accommodation also helps adults and children who use wheelchairs to access services comfortably.

Adjusting the physical environment enhances young children's perception of the reference librarian and encourages the development of social competence. The librarian is seen as an approachable, supportive adult who is available to help them find what they need in the library. A separate section of the reference desk should be high enough to allow adults to rest such items as packs, purses, and packages out of reach of toddlers.

# Noise Level

Monitoring and containing noise is a consideration within the area for young children. There are several interrelated aspects of noise level. Noise enters the library from the surrounding neighborhood and from equipment and people within the library. Communities differ in their ambient noise level. Public libraries are rarely protected from such persistent sources of noise as transportation (traffic, trains, subways, and airplanes) and construction or maintenance (heavy equipment including lawn-care services). Adults and children entering the library are not always conscious of their own volume level. Noise originating in the children's area can impact traditionally quiet areas of the library.

Continuous exposure to noisy environments has a more long-lasting effect on young children than on older children and adults. For example, children living or going to school in areas with high noise levels are found to score lower on standardized tests of intellectual ability than children from similar socioeconomic level in quieter classrooms or housing (McAndrew 1993). While young children generally have little control over the noise level of their home or group setting, excess noise interferes with both verbal and nonverbal communication and learning. For infants, imitation of gestures decreases with high noise levels in the home.

Long-term exposure to high noise levels is associated with increased fatigue, distractibility, and learned helplessness (Wohlwill and Heft 1987). It interferes with the spontaneity of social interaction and instruction as well as the ability to gain information through peripheral learning. Unpredictable noise interrupts activity. Therefore, it is important to shelter the children's area from steady and continuous noise, particularly outside noise above 50–60 decibels, the level of normal conversation.

Nevertheless, it is developmentally appropriate for young children to be exuberant and to fill space with their sounds as well as with their bodies. Provisions for both quiet and noisy activity areas are integral parts of the design of a young children's area. Accommodation needs to be made both for areas of quiet sharing and reflection and for space where the sound of children's exploration and manipulation of objects can be matched by the raised voices of their enthusiasm. Ideally, a separate room can be available for special programs for young children.

# Lighting

The lighting in a room impacts the total emotional climate and the ease of performing tasks. Not only does the light itself influence behavior but an individual's perception of the quality of light can influence his or her feelings about a setting. People associate different types of light with different settings and situations to the extent that light can signal the types of expected behavior. For example, low-level lighting is commonly assumed to be conducive to intimate conversations, whereas bright light is thought to contribute to both feelings of tension and high levels of energy. Bright light has sometimes been associated with increased levels of productivity. These ideas are embedded in the folk wisdom that reduced light calms while bright light increases activity.

Although windowless rooms are common in large buildings and institutional settings, individuals of all ages have a strong preference for natural lighting, agreeing that daylight improves their moods. Daylight frequently enters a room from the side, providing a directional component to the light. Directional light lends interest to three-dimensional details in contrast to the uniform light created by fluorescent lighting. This varied appearance of shadows and shading can assist infant's depth perception learning (Snow 1998).

Fluorescent lighting tends to be less expensive than other forms of lighting but it has also been associated with headaches and eyestrain (Veitch and Gifford 1996), increased fatigue and irritability, and other health concerns (McAndrew 1993). While the relative problems of fluorescent lighting are debated, research continues on the benefits of full-spectrum lighting, which more closely approximates daylight. Full-spectrum light approximates the range of wavelengths available through natural outdoor light, including both the ultraviolet and infrared portions of the spectrum. Full-spectrum light has been credited for increased levels of academic achievement in children (McAndrew, 1993).

Lighting as well as color and thematic materials can be used to define activity and interest centers. Flexibility in lighting, including directional change and dimming capabilities, is important for activities or programs as well as individual patron or staff needs.

Young children rarely spend all day in the library but the experience is enhanced by a view of the outside, especially if they spend several hours in the library setting. The outside view is an important source of stimulation and information. An outside view provides information about times of the day, seasons, and the varied activities of the surrounding neighborhood. It integrates the library with the neighborhood. Building windows at a child's eye level or using seats, platforms, or furniture near secure, durable, and shatter-resistant windows are alternative design solutions that enhance the sense of spaciousness.

## Use of the Room

Room design and the arrangement of furniture and equipment should take into consideration the cycles of use within the young children's area. Sufficient furniture and seating scaled to young children need to meet the demand of the busiest times. Duplication of materials, multiple activity areas, and alternate staffing arrangements help to eliminate a feeling of crowding and the concomitant change in the social and emotional climate of the library.

The psychological sense of crowding is related to the number of people who use a setting and to the access to resources, the number of people in view, and the frequency of social interactions. Crowding is generally associated with more incidents of aggressive behavior for both children and adults. It creates situations in which parents are more apt to use physical restraints and behavior to control the actions of their own children. Not only do crowded settings generate higher noise levels and more behavioral interruptions, they also require the institution of more rules and restrictions. Children who live in chronically crowded conditions have been found to exercise choice less frequently even when given options (Wohlwill and Heft 1987). In high-density residential areas, it may be particularly important for young children and families to find alternative learning areas available in the library and to have opportunities for practicing active decision making.

## Displays and Decorations

A young child's first reaction to a library setting is determined by the sense of place and the messages of welcome. The entryway, the placement of the young children's area, the availability of facilities such as rest rooms with changing facilities, and the nature of family programming and services all convey a message.

Visual characteristics as height, centrality, and arrangement of barriers and pathways have historical, cultural, and personal connections with symbolic and emotional meaning. High ceilings create a sense of openness that can be either inspiring or frightening. Items or displays placed on high shelves or ledges convey the message that they are not available for use. Books on shelves that are above one's head can easily be overlooked or even avoided. Raised platforms, chairs, or service areas require young children and some adults to look up to the individuals ensconced in these locations, creating a sense of social as well as physical distance.

Place identity is a part of personal identity created from a child's experience, familiarity, and confidence with physical places and objects. Messages embedded in the displays and decorations mark an area of the library as a place for young children and contribute to the young child's sense of belonging. Decorating walls and corners with pictures and objects of interest to young children helps them to recognize an area as their own. Memories of the place and past experiences in the setting enter into each child's personal sense of identity and of competence.

Displays of young children's artwork can become landmarks for negotiating the library and for finding the sections and materials of interest and importance. The recognition and use of external landmarks and the pathways between them mark one of the earliest achievements in the development of environmental cognition. Both the identification of one's work as worthy of display and the ability to use art and displays as landmarks offer the young child opportunities to develop a sense of competence. Knowing that one is competent creates self-esteem.

In addition to providing messages of welcome and landmarks for independent movement, displays convey information about programs and services, as well as guidelines for behavior. Information about programs, services, and special collections for young children and their families needs to be visible and accessible. Signs and handouts should contain information about expected library behavior for both adults and children, including a clear statement of behavior guidelines, limits, and responsibilities of all ages. These messages need to be in the languages that will best assist community members and patrons.

Artwork and displays serve other teaching functions. They communicate cultural variation and expression, introduce topics of interest for parents and children, and encourage investigation. It is important that they be free of gender and cultural stereotypes.

Educational and artistic displays showcase community accomplishments and resources. While creating displays and selecting art for decorative purposes, it is important to keep in mind that children's preferences are influenced by both subject matter and presentation. Infants and young children are attracted by bright primary colors, patterns of strong contrast, and things that move.

Young children frequently notice details that are overlooked by adults. The youngest children may show some preference for nonobjective images due to their lack of symbol recognition (Kerlavage 1995). Comments and verbalizations about works of nonobjective art generally refer back to their perceived content. Once children begin to recognize symbols in their own creations, the subject and theme of art and the child's ability to identify realistic aspects of the images become more prominent.

Nevertheless, design elements are not lost on young children. Even children as young as three years old explore design elements such as symmetry, harmony, and repetition in their own two- and three-dimensional creations (Nicolopoulou 1991). By first and second grade, young children distinguish between a picture, a painting, and a reproduction. Using masterworks of art from a range of cultures and time periods within the early childhood area of the library helps children to incorporate different modes and expression into their place identity.

Decorations and displays model alternative artistic styles that can stimulate children's interest in subject matter and validate their own explorations. Young children respond to art spontaneously. The breadth of their imagination and their ability to appreciate a variety of different artistic approaches are influenced by their learned aesthetic experiences. The quality of the art and illustrations in a children's room can make an important contribution.

The children's section is a premier location for the encouragement of emergent literacy. The development of literacy occurs around print materials as children attempt to construct meaning from the patterns around them. Children gain an understanding of how to construct meaning from print and attempt to use print to communicate. Researchers find that children as young as three years old are print-aware and can tell the difference between letters and pictures or doodles. Displaying meaningful symbols and signs at a young child's eye level within the children's area can be used to create a print-rich environment. The signs assist the child in word recognition and in independent use of the environment and resources.

# Health and Safety

The physical environment of the library should be a model of safe and healthy practices both inside and out. Landscape plantings and decorative interior arrangements should not include any poisonous plants. Policy decisions concerning the use of pesticides should take into account the risks to young children both inside and outside the library. Unconventional use of exterior landscape elements for hiding and climbing is common in children's play. Because infants and young children inhabit an area close to the floor and frequently use the floor for play, exploration, and reading, special attention needs to be paid to interior patterns of air circulation and heat at floor level.

It is important in both older buildings and newly erected structures to ensure that areas are free of hazardous material such as lead paint and asbestos. These pose higher risks for young children than for adults. All equipment and materials that are used by young children need to be kept clean and in excellent working condition. Areas should be reviewed for the existence of potential fire hazards. Alternative exits should be indicated and pathways clear of obstructions. Attention needs to be given to the composition of upholstery, curtains, and permanent decorations and displays. Nonflammable materials are required for curtains and upholstery and low flammability is preferred for any other types of decorations or display materials.

The entire library needs to be kept free of trash, dirt, and garbage of any kind. Patrons should be encouraged to participate in maintaining a clean area by having trash receptacles available, with openings out of a toddler's reach. The same guidelines apply to rest rooms and drinking fountains. Rest rooms near the children's area need to be disinfected daily or more frequently as necessary.

Facilities near the children's area should include toilets, sinks, towel dispensers or dryers, and drinking fountains either low enough for a young child to reach independently or with a stable stepstool available. A diaper-changing platform or surface must be available in both the men's and women's rest rooms.

Library design and staff training should ensure swift and appropriate response to emergencies. Emergency procedures and phone numbers should be posted and understood by staff. Exits and other key locations should have emergency lighting in case of power failure. Staff members need to know the location of a first-aid kit and be aware of simple first-aid treatment including the use of universal precautions when handling blood and bodily fluids. Health and safety issues should be a regular and required part of staff training and development.

## COLLECTIONS

The children's collection is an integral part of the physical environment and needs to contain an ample amount of resources for infants, toddlers, preschoolers, and primary grade children. Materials for in-library use as well as circulation are imperative and librarians must continually search for appropriate and safe materials. Chapter 6 covers collection development as part of administration and lists many professional resources that children's librarians can use as they build their collections.

Librarians need to consider the following types of materials both for in-library use as well as circulation:

> books of various types (board, cloth, oversized)
> books for infants and toddlers
> books for preschoolers
> books for primary grade students
> computer software for preschoolers
> computer software for primary grade children
> computer station with Web site linked to sites targeted to young children
> videos for preschoolers

videos for primary grade children

compact discs, records, and/or cassettes for preschoolers

compact discs, records, and/or cassettes for primary grade children

listening and/or viewing stations

multimedia kits

toys

puzzles and pegboards

art supplies

blocks and building materials

science equipment (e.g., magnifying glass, wall charts, posters, weights)

active play equipment (e.g., climbing equipment, wheel toys, sand/water table)

manipulatives to sort, classify, and label

dramatic play equipment or materials (e.g., dress-up items, dollhouse, puppet stage, puppets and dolls, flannelboard)

In order for children to use these materials in the library, it is best to establish separate spaces or stations. Multimedia learning stations that include computers loaded with preschool software or bookmarked with special Internet sites for young children, an audiovisual corner for video viewing or listening to audiotapes, and/or a parent-child literacy corner with packaged pre-reading and literacy activities entice young children and their parents to access materials within the library environment. These stations or spaces can be created in a separate early childhood area or within sections (computer rooms, program rooms, seating areas) of the children's room.

# ASSESSMENT OF PHYSICAL ENVIRONMENT

Libraries offer services to the community, but first and foremost they provide special spaces in urban, suburban, and rural areas. An understanding of the impact of design, safety, aesthetics, functionality, and the breadth and scope of collections is essential to better practice when serving the youngest patrons.

The physical environment needs to provide a visual and interactive setting for families. How libraries create and support their children's rooms tells the community how they feel about service for this audience. Chapter 1 provides a listing of resources that further assist librarians in developing and evaluating appropriate learning environments for young children (see pp. 12–13).

Assessing the library landscape with reference to appropriate design, lighting, safety, collection diversity, equipment, and comfort is required if a library is to serve young children properly. Specific tools directed to the assessment of the physical environment include forms B-1, B-2, B-5, B-10, C-2, C-6, and D-4.

# REFERENCES

*The Early Childhood Quality Review Initiative for public libraries.* 1995. Centereach, N.Y.: Middle Country Public Library.

Kerlavage, M. 1995. A bunch of naked ladies and a tiger: Children's responses to adult works of art. In *The visual arts and early childhood learning*, ed. C. Thompson. Reston, Va.: The National Art Education Association.

McAndrew, F. T. 1993. *Environmental psychology.* Pacific Grove, Calif.: Brooks/Cole.

Moore, G. 1987. The physical environment and cognitive development in child-care centers. In *Spaces for children: The built environment and child development,* ed. C. Weinstein, and T. David. New York: Plenum.

Nicolopoulou, A. 1991. Constructive play: A window into the mind of the preschooler. In *Play and social context of development in early care and education* by B. Scales et. al., 173–91. New York: Teachers College Press.

Olds, A. 1987. Designing settings for infants and toddlers. *Spaces for children: The built environment and child development,* ed. C. Weinstein, and T. David. New York: Plenum.

Snow, C. 1998. *Infant development,* 2nd ed. Upper Saddle River, N.J.: Prentice-Hall.

Veitch, J., and R. Gifford. 1996. Assessing beliefs about lighting effects on health performance, mood, and social behavior. *Environment and Behavior* 28, no. 4: 446–70.

Wohlwill, J., and H. Heft. 1987. The physical environment and the development of the child. In *Handbook of environmental psychology,* ed. D. Stokols and I. Altman. New York: Wiley.

# 4

# Parent Participation

Central to the provision of library service for young children is the recognition of the family's importance. Communication between librarians and parents is based on the concept that parents and family are the principal influences in a child's life and that the library is there to extend and enrich this lifelong dialogue. Parents, not professionals, are the "constant" figures for children. Librarians must focus on what they can do to support parents in their multifaceted roles as primary caregivers and first teachers. If they are to meet the needs of young children effectively, librarians must acknowledge and validate complex parental roles and accept the unique perspectives of parents as partners in the library mission. A family centered library is an outgrowth of the genuine belief that parents can and should contribute to the development of library services.

The participation of parents is the hallmark of high quality early childhood programs. Librarians need to listen to parents. The reaction of parents to programs, their insights into their children's behavior and the behavior of staff and volunteers, and their ideas about library policies, future programs, and resource development are important contributions. Communication needs to flow in both directions. Building the parent-professional partnership is a necessary ingredient of every aspect of library service for young children.

When parents are welcomed as partners, contributors, observers, participants, and collaborators, their presence and expertise enrich the program and the library. They, in turn, become better informed about the breadth of library and community resources and the particulars of their own children's development. Including parents in early childhood programs and program planning reaps benefits for individuals, families, and the community. It fosters adult development, nurturing a growing confidence and competence in parenting and in community advocacy for young children.

It is essential for children's librarians to form a partnership with parents to effectively plan, implement, prioritize, and evaluate services for young children. Partnerships based on a common interest, need for action, and sense of mutuality enhance joint efforts. Trust and confidence in the library reinforce the community's image of the library as an institution committed to families and young children. Partnerships grow out of mutual respect.

Sharing knowledge nurtures the development of mutual respect and understanding. It is facilitated through the use and elaboration of multiple communication pathways. Although one-way communication from the library to parents through newsletters, bibliographies, and handouts is important, librarians need to look for avenues that encourage both communication from parents to the library and an active exchange among all library stakeholders, including parents.

## PARENTS AS CRITICAL FRIENDS

The business community has long recognized the necessity of consumer input to build its customer base and product image. Quality library-based early childhood programs reflect a user-oriented and customer-driven approach to public library service. Through this approach, services are designed and evaluated based on patron input. Seeking parent input creates a new image of children's services and identifies "the better and the best" practices affecting families and their access to library services.

Highly visible and attractive suggestion boxes or log books are typical vehicles for encouraging communication from clients. One of the best techniques to encourage parent input and participation is the use of focus groups designed around particular issues. Focus groups provide librarians with the opportunity to view library services through the eyes of parents who use the library and, if effectively conducted, generate a bond between the librarian and the parent participant. By conducting focus groups, librarians become more customer oriented.

Focus groups are usually made up of supportive families (families that use the library) so the librarian has a chance to learn from "critical friends." Focus groups can help sort out the confusion that surrounds a service and the issues that must be addressed.

Parent interviews, program evaluations, and parent surveys are other practical methods for improving services. Individual parent interviews may be more difficult to conduct in the library setting than focus groups. Sometimes parents feel uncomfortable relaying messages about library service, particularly if asked specific questions that may result in ambivalent or potentially negative responses. Distributing questions before the interview or using nonstaff interviewers are possible ways to alleviate discomfort.

A written questionnaire or survey, filled out while the parent uses the children's room or the preschool child attends a story time, may generate a more positive and thought-provoking response from parents. Parent surveys are a simple method for obtaining relevant input. Like focus group questions, interview or survey questions must be well designed to gather useful information.

An evaluation questionnaire at the end of a program is one form of survey that is an excellent vehicle for eliciting timely and useful information from parents. This brief set of questions can be distributed to parents at the end of a program. Program evaluations can become part of regular library service and can be saved for inclusion in the library's portfolio.

Implementing the Early Childhood Quality Review affords the library an excellent opportunity to reach out and engage parents in the development of children's services for families. Although the prospect of an entire review may seem overwhelming, components of the review are critical to achieving success. Parent focus groups and parent interviews are a part of the review process. They can be used to assess individual elements such as children's programs or the social environment. They are also an effective strategy to begin the parent participation process in the library setting.

## PARENTS AS ADVOCATES

Although soliciting parental suggestions and staff understanding of a parental perspective is essential to the development of library services for young children and their families, of equal importance is the provision of opportunities for the development of an ongoing dialog. Individual parents may be valuable volunteers and/or members of the Friends or the library board. Their active presence at site visits, at meetings with other community agencies, or with potential program funders may enhance the library's presentation. Parents may feel that it is an honor to be asked to participate in these and other "behind-the-scenes" aspects of the library.

When parents participate on committees, advisory and policy-making boards such as Friends' organizations, or the library's board of trustees, they are embarking on a path of collaboration, a two-way communication. From this position, they are able to exchange information with librarians, staff, and administrators.

In addition to providing feedback on programs and services, parents gain a better understanding of the resources and constraints influencing the initiation and support of library services. Speaking out on services for young children and their families from within these organizations and at government meetings promotes and emphasizes the importance of library service for children. The presence of parents at this level makes a clear statement about their value to the institution. It is from this vantage point that parent leaders may galvanize a community to action.

Since programs and areas of participation differ in the degree to which parental involvement is integral to their mission and activity, it is important that both parents and staff have a clear understanding of responsibilities and expectations. For many parents membership on library advisory boards, committees, or evaluation teams will be a "first" experience of this nature. In order to avoid confusion and misunderstandings that could undermine the development of a working partnership, parents need to receive appropriate information about time commitments, goals, roles, meeting agendas, and program structure in a timely manner. It is important to present this in a manner free of jargon, both orally and in writing, before the beginning of each session, workshop, or meeting. Some parents may need encouragement to participate at this level. They may need training in the culture of the library as an institution and its relationship to other community agencies and services.

Collaborating with parents to improve library and community services for children is a relatively new concept for children's librarians. However, parents are powerful allies. Forming an alliance can be a boon for children's services in a public library. The idea of family-provider partnerships is synonymous with better practice. It supports and enhances library-based early childhood service.

In communities where libraries are supported directly through a public vote, parents become an important constituency for the library. They can ensure that budget appropriations take into consideration the needs of young children and their families and that monetary resources are appropriately allocated to address these needs. Parents of young children can be encouraged to vote in the library election and will often get other parents to vote. This political process is vital for building a constituency for children's services.

Providing good service is the library's best method for attracting and developing advocates. Parents who regularly use the library and the early childhood programs spread the word about this community resource, bringing friends, neighbors, and relatives into the library. Active participants and patrons often give regular feedback to staff regarding programs and collections. Building relationships with young children and their families is in the best interest of children's services. It is a way of nurturing generations of library enthusiasts.

## PARENTS AS PARTNERS IN THE EDUCATIONAL PROCESS

As partners, the librarian and parent pool their knowledge to facilitate the learning process for the child. This involves identifying library programs and services that are of interest to the parent and/or child, locating community and library resources that parents may need to guide and educate their children, or introducing a range of written, manipulative, visual, or auditory materials to satisfy the child's and/or parent's needs. Helping parents understand their child's unique process of discovery learning and emergent literacy, providing appropriately designed programs that target both parents and children, and designing the environment using the best materials available are examples of the role of the librarian as educator and facilitator.

The design of children's programs, the opportunity for one-on-one interactions, and a diverse selection of activities and resources provide parents with a range of opportunities to observe the scope of children's learning styles, approaches, and timetables. The librarian's acceptance of diversity and individual differences enables parents to better understand their own child. Alternative approaches to specific situations can be suggested in a nonjudgmental manner.

The librarian is an outsider to the family dynamic and brings an objective perspective into interactions with both the child and the parent. Library staff and program personnel can help parents observe their child's behavior and can provide reassurance and information about typical developmental stages.

Understanding the feelings of parents and empathizing with their particular situation is of utmost importance in establishing trust and forging a partnership. Effective communication between parents and the librarian is based on active and reflective listening skills, mutual respect, the ability to respond to nonverbal messages, and a willingness to explore alternatives. These communication techniques need to be part of each interaction and practiced regularly. Information may need to be made available in languages other than English for parents and grandparents for whom English is a second language. Other adults and children with special communication disabilities may need technical assistance or specialized materials to ensure effective communication.

## Linking Parents to Resources

It is important to present the library as a path to information and services without implying that librarians have the solutions to interpersonal problems, particularly when talking with a parent about a concern or issue. As an educator, a librarian describes observed behavior or offers information about typical development. Conducting a professional reference interview and locating information for parents on any one of the many child-rearing issues of today underscore the work of the public librarian working in children's services.

Picture books and videos can help parents better understand and approach young children concerning emotional issues and even provide insight into typical child behavior. Librarians need to be aware of children's materials that can assist parents with everyday as well as sensitive or difficult issues. A general knowledge of issue-oriented picture books is important for librarians and staff working with young children and their families.

Libraries need an array of good bibliographies and a sampling of the recommended picture books with effective cataloging to facilitate access to these titles. *Books to Help Children Cope with Separation and Loss* (Rudman et al. 1993) is an excellent bibliography which can help to access picture books dealing with such topics as the death of a grandparent or parental divorce. *A to Zoo: Subject Access to Children's Picture Books* (1993) and *The Bookfinder: A Guide to Children's Literature about the Needs and Problems of Youth Aged 2–15* (1994) are two other excellent sources listing books for young children that deal with sensitive issues.

Direct counseling on the actions, expectations, or options appropriate for an individual child or family requires a different type of expertise. Library staff and program personnel can help parents to observe their child's behavior, providing reassurance and information about typical developmental stages. However, if a parent needs a counselor, the librarian's role is to acknowledge the need and act as an information resource professional providing referral choices that address the need. Chapter 5 describes the librarian's role as an information and referral provider.

During the field testing of the *Early Childhood Quality Review Initiative for Public Libraries* (1995), reviewers noted that referrals can occur in the context of library programs such as the Parent/Child Workshop (Feinberg and Deerr 1995). "Verbal cuing by the librarians and staff, to inform and prepare parents about resource people visiting the program, upcoming activities, available resources, program goals etc., empowers parents to approach and utilize the resource persons most effectively (appropriate questions to ask, language to use), and lets them take the lead concerning issues regarding their own child" (Notes, MCPL 15).

## SUPPORTING ADULTS IN THEIR ROLE AS PARENTS

Parenthood requires a range of skills and knowledge for which most adults are minimally prepared. Without formal preparation for the tasks of parenting, most adults attempt to handle each parenting task to the best of their ability given the totality of their life experiences and current pressures. Parenting is a minute-by-minute proposition, occurring "between the lines" as well as at easily recognizable junctures. Learning is also a daily affair for children and their parents. Yet the small successes and accomplishments that provide the texture of everyday parenting are rarely acknowledged in a society that is quick to criticize less than perfect outcomes.

Parents need encouragement. Their steps toward enhancing their own skills and those of their children need acknowledgment and praise. Librarians can provide positive support and join parents in their daily struggle to raise children. Library programs for infants, toddlers, and young children provide an opportunity for librarians to involve parents in their children's learning and to mentor adults in their roles as parents.

Special programs that are designed to facilitate parent-child interactions support the parent's teaching role. Librarians can encourage parents to take an active role in their child's earliest experiences and to be involved in their child's development. It is exciting for parents to recognize learning in their child. Observing their infant listening intently to a nursery rhyme or hearing their toddler ask for "Open, Shut Them" during circle time amazes parents who may not be engaged in these activities at home. Often parents tell librarians about the child who does not do fingerplays during story time, but repeats them verbatim when driving home from the library.

Story time or nursery rhyme programs for parents and children are opportunities to demonstrate to parents language enrichment strategies while enhancing mutual learning. This approach places equal emphasis on developing the skills of parents and on the language development of the child. Participating in Mother Goose or story time educates parents on the "what and how" of repeating rhymes and stories.

Sometimes parents feel uncomfortable acting "silly" and using playful verbal and body language. They may not have observed emotionally expressive storytelling or considered this type of interaction as part of their parental role. Many parents are isolated from their own extended families and do not recall finger games or favorite books. Libraries and librarians can support the idea that having fun together can enhance the learning experience and set the foundation for a positive relationship throughout life.

One member of a field site review team, in observing a "Mostly Mother Goose" program, commented on the interaction and the participation: "The impact is greater on the parent who learns how to interact with their children" (Notes, PML 10). Parents who were interviewed acknowledged the mutual learning process. One parent, commenting on a positive aspect of the early childhood library program, pointed out: "Parents are able to learn right along with their child and learn in a fun way too" (Notes, SPL 8).

The early learning environment in a library setting can teach parents through example about appropriate toys and other play materials, as well as provide a model of a child-centered and safe setting. Libraries have a wonderful opportunity to expose parents to well-designed equipment and materials, including early learning software. Parents learn from librarians where to purchase toys and ask to borrow special catalogs of early learning materials that are not typically promoted to the home market.

Sharing a story, talking about favorite characters, and discussing feelings and ideas are integral to engaging young children and parents in the learning process. Librarians can create an atmosphere that helps parents to feel comfortable with a range of language-rich interactive styles. They provide examples of songs, games, and stories from around the world that can assist parents in finding a personal play vocabulary. Parents are often surprised by what their child can and will do when involved in a new experience.

The librarian sets an example for parents by guiding a child through a project (or an activity) rather than doing it for the child. When "library staff provides information to parents during art activities in a variety of programs, explain[ing] the significance of the process and encourag[ing] parents to explore different mediums and continue the activities at home, [it] reinforces the parent's role as their child's first teacher" (Notes, MCPL 5). The combination of new strategies and renewed feelings of confidence empowers parents in their teaching role.

Talking with parents before and after programs is a good time to emphasize the parents' importance in the child's learning. Materials directed toward parents that help extend the learning experience for them, as well as for the child, need to be made available at each program. The carryover from the library to home is an important part of the sequential learning that is stimulated by the library experience. Providing support and encouragement to parents helps them to better understand developmentally appropriate practices that facilitate learning for infants and young children in the library, in child-care or preschool settings, and at home.

Librarians need to focus their energies on enabling successful and satisfied parents. Helping parents to understand and appreciate their own child's strengths and needs is a key aspect of good library service. By integrating parents' and children's services and providing a continuum of parent-involvement programs for infants, toddlers, and preschoolers, librarians can let parents observe firsthand how their child learns and adapts to a variety of situations. Knowledge and acceptance of one's own child are fundamental to the parent's role as teacher.

Educating and informing parents about child development and encouraging the use of library services to bolster emergent literacy, reading readiness, and social development through child-child and adult-child interactions are primary tasks of the children's librarian. Library programs for young children are often a child's first social experience. Through these programs, parents not only view their child's learning style but they gain insights into the way their child approaches new social encounters. Focusing on the social aspects of learning, librarians model for parents alternative strategies for resolving social conflicts. Parents are more likely to adopt these practices at home once they have observed their successful use within a library program.

# PARENT EDUCATION AND SUPPORT

In the midst of everyday hassles, adults frequently make parenting decisions based on memories of their own childhood and the collective wisdom of extended family. Although schools are acknowledged guardians of information about children and education, these institutions are also in a position to evaluate children and, by extension, their families. Many parents have uneasy memories of their own school experiences, however, and are reluctant or ambivalent in seeking answers to questions about parenting from school officials.

Libraries, on the other hand, are neutral, safe, and, ideally, associated with positive feelings and impressions. Providing services for young children and their parents helps both of these generations turn to the library as an important community resource to facilitate learning. Building competence and confidence in parents is a primary goal of the partnership model.

In constructing a quality early childhood service program, children's librarians need to recognize parents as adult learners. By serving the parent as an individual, not only as part of the family unit, librarians create and maintain a parent's trust, promoting mutual learning about the child and his or her needs. This parent component encompasses the facilitation of informal parent-to-parent learning, the maintenance of an informal support role, and the presentation of opportunities for structured education and training.

# Informal Learning

Friendships formed by parents who repeatedly meet at library programs designed for their children are an important part of the social fabric of parenthood. While participating in library programs or visiting the library to check out materials with their young children, parents identify others at a similar stage in life. They recognize others with children the age of their own. These parents and families are potential friends not only for the adults but for the children. These meetings may initiate the start of play groups, cooperative child-care arrangements, clothing and equipment swaps, and even more formal support groups or networks.

Through these informal meetings, parents have the opportunity to exchange information and advice. They are able to observe a range of abilities and behaviors in children of similar ages, and to assess the style and sometimes the efficacy of a variety of parenting strategies. Parents have few situations that allow for these types of casual learning opportunities.

As they follow housing and work opportunities, many parents have had to say good-bye permanently or temporarily to work-based friendships, familiar neighborhoods, and extended families. Young parents often begin the process of parenthood in relative isolation. As new parents, they seek new companions to share this stage of life and responsibility. Libraries and librarians can help alleviate this sense of isolation.

The best practices identified during the field testing support the importance of the informal learning that occurs at libraries when adults make a parent-to-parent connection. One parent reported: "Young parents talk to each other; helping each other" (Notes, SPL 12). Others related: "Parents learned many parenting tips from the library's programs and from other parents that they met in the programs, many of whom developed friendships as a result of their library connection" (Notes, MCPL 13). "I feel [the library does] a fabulous job! I know it's hard to do too much for the children under $1^1/_2$ years old, but I also know first-time Moms with very young children sometimes need some extra support, especially those new to the community" (Notes, SPL 16).

# Parent Education Programs

Casual learning within the library setting, while critical to family learning, is not always enough for parents. In many situations parents need more direct avenues for their education and development. During interviews and focus groups, parents often requested workshops on specific topics such as how to use pre-reading and math materials; things to do in the area for children of different ages; instructional workshops on educational software; selecting good literature for children; child development issues such as toilet training and sleep problems; and discipline techniques (*Early Childhood Quality Review* 1995).

Providing parent education and support groups that deal with a wide range of parenting challenges and dilemmas is an essential part of early childhood programming. These can be facilitated to enable parents to learn not only from the library staff but also from each other.

## Program format

Designing a program series for parents underscores the children's librarian's acceptance of serving adults in their parenting role. Parents learn best when their knowledge and needs are respected. Using a variety of real-life situations to illustrate the issue or to stimulate discussion engages parents in active problem solving and assists them in relating topics to their own family and circumstances. The development of a positive emotional climate within the program or workshop allows parents the opportunity to identify those aspects of information and parenting strategies that best fit their own needs (Involving Families in Advisory Roles 1994).

The adults who take part in any particular parent education workshop, program, or series usually come from a range of backgrounds and experiences. Depending on the focus and meeting location, there may be a diversity of ages, cultures, socioeconomic levels, and interests, as well as social and language skills. Expectations may vary widely. Some parents may be more familiar with group discussion formats; others with settings in which an authority figure hands down information. For this reason, it is important that programs be offered in a range of formats, and that ground rules for the communication and sharing of ideas, thoughts, and experiences be made explicit from the beginning. Oral and written presentation of this information, along with a clear description of program goals and structure, can facilitate the group process.

In order for programs to be successful, participants need to feel comfortable in expressing their feelings, voicing their concerns, and offering examples of their successes. Simple strategies such as name tags and "ice breakers" that encourage individuals to talk with each other can be employed to encourage individuals to feel comfortable in the group setting and to identify with group goals.

Since not all adults have had the opportunity to talk about their feelings or to practice public speaking or respectful listening, initial meetings of some programs may need to devote time to the development of communication skills. The sessions themselves may be designed to explore alternative approaches to information and group exchange such as brainstorming, role playing of family or group roles, dramatizations, short lectures, debates, and open discussions. Other parent education formats include book discussions and reviews and even previews of children's or parent's educational and recreational videos or computer programs.

Experts or professionals may be brought to the library from the community for individual sessions or as members of a panel or symposium. They can be joined by individuals offering the parent perspective on the issue. Alternatively, either parents or members of the library staff may act as moderators who can pose questions from their own perspective, read questions submitted prior to the program, or solicit and select questions from the audience. A variant of this format offers two parallel panels, a panel of experts and one of parents.

Oftentimes, these programs can be designed cooperatively with other community agencies. The library may supply meeting space and publicity. Visiting parents in other local settings to talk about the library's resources can be another avenue for reaching this targeted audience. Chapter 5 focuses on outreach efforts as part of family centered services.

Each of these formats requires a slightly different room arrangement. The physical arrangement of chairs and tables influences the flow of conversation and provides messages about the formality of expected social interactions. The space between furniture and the nature of the decorations provide cues for behavior and influence whether parents expect the tone to be formal, as in a theater, classroom, or boardroom, or informal, as in a living room or lounge area.

Cross-cultural studies confirm that side-by-side seating is considered the most intimate of seating arrangements (McAndrew 1993). However, this arrangement may have an inhibiting effect on conversation, whereas furnishings that encourage corner-to-corner or face-to-face interactions may facilitate exchanges. These physical structures encode expectations for social interaction. For this reason, such factors as the location of visual aids, lights, and microphones; the hardness or softness of the furniture; and the shape of tables and the grouping of chairs around them should be taken into consideration when selecting a meeting location.

## Learning styles

In designing parent education programs, it is important to keep in mind that adults have a range of preferred learning styles. Visual, auditory, and, where appropriate, tactile materials should be incorporated into program design. Opportunities to interact in large and small groups should be considered during the planning process. Handouts, brochures, and bibliographies are a positive addition to these events, as are concrete examples of home-based applications. Some series of workshops incorporate take-home assignments to encourage parent exploration of new parenting techniques as well as participation in group discussion.

Whenever possible, books and audio and video materials from the parents' collection relevant to the program should be available for parents to borrow and take home with them. This may involve securing sufficient copies of key resources, as well as items in alternative formats for parents with special needs or those who are learning English as a second language. Materials from the children's collection can also be included to encourage that the learning that begins in the program will be explored at home. An evaluation component is a critical part of parent education workshops. Librarians should set aside time to talk to parents both before and after programs.

Building in a social time during or after parent education programs can facilitate the development of informal support networks. Parents who meet to discuss child-rearing issues are able to use this opportunity to make friends and identify individuals with similar interests and perspectives. Those parents who hesitate to take part in a parent workshop or program may find network participation a more satisfying vehicle for developing friendships and gaining advice. They may be attracted to the informal one-on-one aspects of a network rather than the group environment of a parenting program or they may prefer the flexibility of connecting as needed rather than keeping to a fixed schedule.

Libraries need to initiate or facilitate the development of a parent support network as distinct from the parent education programs. One format is a parent mentor program that matches first-time parents with more experienced parents who can provide alternative models of child rearing and information about local customs and resources. Both formal and informal parent support programs provide opportunities for adults to broaden their social connections. These networks of peer relationships among adults can enhance the emotional climate within families.

## Parents' Collection

One of the most effective ways to provide education and support for parents is through the establishment of a parents' collection. Types of materials include books, videos, audio books, periodicals, electronic resources, and pamphlets. Information on child development, reading and literature, activities for young children, health and nutrition, music and art education, child rearing, and children with special needs helps parents to better understand their role in the learning process.

Attractively packaging and locating these materials encourage the use of this collection. Kits can be assembled that offer an array of materials on special topics such as going to the hospital, death and dying, sibling relationships, and having a new baby, or that build connections between books and a range of activities focusing on current or classical children's interests. These kits are not only successful with parents but are attractive to grandparents and family home day-care providers.

Having Web sites bookmarked with Internet resources on child development and parenting provides parents with current child-rearing information and indirectly strengthens their computer literacy skills. It is not uncommon for parents to first use a computer in the children's room. Encouraging parents to join their young children in the computer area and having resources specifically earmarked for them as well as their children afford the children's librarian an opportunity to foster family computer literacy.

Based on a list developed by Barbara Jordan (1996), parents need information on an array of topics, including:

child development (mental, physical, social, and emotional)

common childhood illnesses

discipline and parenting skills

infant care and child rearing

language and reading activities

nutrition and physical fitness

speech and language development

children's fears

toilet training

home schooling

sleep problems

emotional disorders of childhood

children and the media

death and bereavement

home and school issues

working parents

developmentally appropriate activities for children

divorce, single parent, gay family, and stepfamily issues

communication and family relationships

family travel and recreation

safety and health

parenting children with special needs

sibling relationships

pregnancy and prenatal care

stress and depression in children

sexuality education

children's parties

children's toys, furniture, rooms, and equipment

adolescent issues

child abuse and family dysfunction

adoption and foster care

alcohol and substance abuse

specific health and disability topics

Traditional methods of promoting collections and resources also help to alert parents to the availability of library materials directed to their parenting needs. Bibliographies, resource displays, and exhibits on parenting issues provide adults with suggestions of other community settings where information is available. When arranging the parents' collection, it is important to keep in mind that these materials need to be in close proximity to or accessible within the children's area (Lobosco et al. 1996; Jordan 1996). Collection visibility, special publications, and displays make a statement about the importance of parents in the growth process of children. They serve as reminders to parents that children's librarians can help them with their parent education needs.

## PARENT/PROFESSIONAL COLLECTIONS AND SERVICES
### Selected Resources

Bredekamp, S. 1987. *Developmentally appropriate practice in early childhood programs serving children from birth through age eight.* Washington, D.C.: National Association for the Education of Young Children.

Carpenter, K. H. 1995. *Sourcebook on parenting and child care.* Phoenix, Ariz.: Oryx Press.

Cohen, B. P., and L. S. Simkin. 1994. *Library-based parent resource centers: A guide to implementing programs.* Albany, N.Y.: New York Developmental Disabilities Planning Council and the New York Library Association.

DeFrancis, B. 1994. *The parents' resource almanac.* Holbrook, Mass.: Bob Adams, Inc.

Feinberg, S., and K. Deerr. 1995. *Running a parent/child workshop.* New York: Neal-Schuman.

Feinberg, S., and S. Feldman. 1996. *Serving families and children through partnerships.* New York: Neal-Schuman.

Feinberg, S., et al. 1998. *Including families and children with special needs.* New York: Neal-Schuman.

Greene, E. 1991. *Books, babies, and libraries: Serving infants, toddlers, their parents and caregivers.* Chicago: American Library Association.

Haskins, R. 1981. *Parent education and public policy: A conference report.* Summary of conference on "Parent Education and Public Policy" (Durham, N.C., March 1980) Washington, D.C.: National Institute of Education.

Interagency Work Group on Parent Education and Support. nd. *New York parents: Guiding principles and core service components for parent education and support programs.* Albany, N.Y.: Council of Children and Families.

Jordan, B., and N. Stackpole. 1994. *Audiovisual resources for family programming.* New York: Neal-Schuman.

Lobosco, A. F., et al. 1996. Serving families in the community: Library-based parent resource centers. *Public Libraries* (September/October): 298–305.

Nuba, H., M. Searson, and D. L. Sheiman, eds. 1994. *Resources for early childhood: A handbook.* New York: Garland.

*Partners for inclusion: Welcoming infants and toddlers with disabilities and their families into community activities: A resource guide.* 1997. Hauppauge, New York: Suffolk County Department of Health Services.

Steele, B., and C. Willard. 1989. *Guidelines for establishing a family resource library.* 2nd ed. Washington, D.C.: Association for the Care of Children's Health.

Thurling, J. 1994. *Serving families with limited resources: Selected resources for providers of parent education.* Canandaigua, N.Y.: Cornell Cooperative Extension of Ontario County.

# PARENTS AS LIFELONG LEARNERS

Serving parents is critical to the future of children's services in public libraries. Interacting with the parent as an adult learner and recognizing the information needs of parents enhance the role of the children's librarian within the library as well as in the greater community of family support professionals. When the librarian forms a relationship with the parent, she or he facilitates lifelong learning within the family unit and underscores the value of educating the parent to educate the child.

A basic thrust of library-based early childhood service is the active involvement of parents in all aspects of the library. In the public library setting, infants, toddlers, preschoolers, and early elementary school-age children are usually accompanied by family members or child-care providers. This affords the librarian an extraordinary opportunity to promote the library during the child's earliest learning years. Through the active participation of a parent or caregiving adult, librarians facilitate an exponential learning process that begins with the parent/child dyad.

Children's librarians need to be familiar with the entire range of adult services and seek opportunities to inform parents as potential users. Adults who may first enter the library to entertain their child or to enlarge their social group begin to expand their own educational horizons. Information for adults within the secure early childhood setting may woo a reluctant adult into investigating additional library resources directed primarily to adult interests and needs. This sets in motion a cycle of continuous learning for all family members.

Family literacy programs can often be incorporated within the domain of the children's services department. Librarians need to seek out effective programs and adapt them to the library environment. This type of service usually requires that the librarian collaborate with another local agency that has access to parents who cannot read or who have low literacy skills. Using computer software that emphasizes reading readiness and emergent literacy skills in the library and encouraging parents to attend story times with their children allow libraries to help parents as well as children become literate.

# ASSESSMENT OF PARENT PARTICIPATION

Parent participation is best evaluated using methodology designed to assess the attitudes and perceptions of parents and professionals. Interviews, focus groups, surveys and questionnaires are useful tools. Additional information can be found by reviewing the library's documents dealing with parent activity, including written program announcements.

When assessing parent participation, it is important to consider their multiple roles. Parents of young children should be recognized as a child's primary teacher; guided in developmentally appropriate practice; encouraged to actively participate in their child's learning; provided opportunities for parent education and support; and viewed as partners in planning and evaluation and as advocates in support of the development of services for families and children. It is helpful to assess services from the point of view of the parent as mentor, teacher, and model of behavior for his or her child as well as that of a direct beneficiary of the library's programs and services.

Specific items in the appendix that apply to parent participation include forms B-1, B-2, B-6, B-12, C-3, C-4, C-5, C-7, D-5, and D-6.

REFERENCES

*A to zoo: Subject access to children's picture books.* 1993. New Providence, R.I.: Bowker.

Berger, H. E. 1991. *Parents as partners in education: The school and home working together.* 3rd ed. New York: Macmillan.

Bernstein, J. E. 1977. *Books to help children cope with separation and loss.* Providence, R.I.: Bowker.

*The bookfinder: A guide to children's literature about the needs and problems of youth aged two–fifteen.* 1994. Circle Pines, Minn.: American Guidance Service.

*Early Childhood Quality Review Initiative for public libraries.* 1995. Centereach, N.Y.: Middle Country Public Library.

Feinberg, S., and K. Deerr. 1995. *Running a Parent/Child Workshop: A how-to-do-it manual for librarians.* New York: Neal-Schuman.

Involving families in advisory roles: Eight steps to success. 1994. In *Essential allies* volume of *Advances in family centered care,* 2–6. Washington, D.C.: Institute for Family-Centered Care.

Jordan, B. 1996. Building a family support collection. Chap. 11 in *Serving families and children through partnerships* by S. Feinberg and S. Feldman. New York: Neal-Schuman.

Lobosco, A. F., et al. 1996. Serving families in the community: Library-based parent resource centers. *Public Libraries* (September/October): 298–305.

MacAndrew, F. T. 1993. *Environmental psychology.* Pacific Grove, Calif.: Brooks/Cole.

Notes from interviews, focus groups, and surveys conducted at the Middle Country Public Library (MCPL), Newburg Public Library (NPL), Patchogue Medford Library (PML) and Shoreham-Wading River Public Library (SPL). *The Early Childhood Quality Review Initiative for public libraries.* Centereach, N.Y.: Middle Country Public Library, 1995.

Rudman, M. K. *Books to help children cope with separation and loss.* New Providence, N.J.: Bowker, 1993.

# 5

# Collaborations and Networks

$A$ truly holistic approach to serving young children and families requires active participation in community networks, partnerships, and collaborations. Providing information and referral, coalition building, outreach, offering reference help to adults who work with young children and families, acquiring interdisciplinary training, and participating in professional organizations are some of the strategies that librarians utilize in their efforts to provide quality service. These strategies, which build upon the library's strengths and respond to the needs of young children and their families, enable the library to claim a position within the early childhood and family support community.

Active and creative involvement among all agencies, including libraries, is necessary in order to maximize community resources for children and families and to close the gaps in the existing service delivery system. Partnerships and collaborations foster the development of new programs and collections within the library and integrate library service with the entire range of family support services. A seamless flow between libraries and preschool programs, and libraries and parent education programs, enables families to make full use of the resources available within the community.

In most situations it is the library personnel who actively choose to seek relationships with other community agencies and organizations. There are several exemplary partnership models currently in use that have effected change and improved library services (Feinberg and Feldman 1996).

The Library–Head Start–Museum Project is an excellent national model designed to share information and resources among librarians, museum educators, and Head Start staff. The library provides a program presenter to Head Start or the museums on selected topics such as storytelling, library skills, and the importance of reading aloud to children. Head Start provides program presenters at libraries and museums on topics such as parent training and child development. The museum provides displays and outreach programs to libraries and Head Start facilities.

The three agencies may put together displays to promote family learning activities to audiences at Head Start, museums, and libraries. Libraries promote books to parents to help prepare them for visits to museums. Head Start brings groups of parents and children to libraries and museums. Each agency has specialized staff to provide training to other staff in their area of expertise.

The Family Place project, a project of Libraries for the Future (New York City) in partnership with Middle Country Public Library (Centereach, New York), is another excellent example of a library-based community collaborative in which the goal is to help libraries become family centered. This privately funded national initiative aims to develop "family places" in the children's rooms of five public libraries. In addition to setting up space, the libraries implement the Parent/Child Workshop and other family-oriented programs, develop parents' collections, build a community coalition around the family place, and reach out to community institutions that work with families. A goal of this model is to systemically change the philosophy of children's services from serving only the child to providing services for parents and family support professionals.

The Suffolk Coalition for Parents and Children in Centereach, New York (on Long Island), is a library-sponsored collaboration at the local level. This organization brings together an array of family service providers and librarians who share information about local programs and services for young children, youth, and families. It puts key players at the same table to communicate about service gaps and needs. Meeting bimonthly for over twenty years, professionals from this coalition have gone on to create innovative and collaborative initiatives including countywide conferences, special task forces, interagency programs and a Community Resource Database. This database involved the work of more than forty of the coalition-affiliated agencies, with one local library acting as central manager.

Librarians in the Suffolk Coalition for Parents and Children are also sought out as grant partners and regularly asked to develop cooperative programs in their local communities. Partners for Inclusion (Feinberg et al. 1998) was a grant partnership that developed between two libraries and two early childhood centers that work with children who have special needs. Designed to integrate families and children with disabilities into typical community programs and settings, this partnership involved the staff from each institution, the county government early intervention team, and a community coalition of interested professionals and parents. Through the development of collaborative strategies, including a circulating adaptive toy collection, to help librarians integrate children with special needs into programs, this project provided support to reluctant families who might otherwise have been too intimidated to use the library.

# INFORMATION AND REFERRAL

The first and most basic component of a holistic family approach is the library's information and referral service. If the community has not initiated the development of a comprehensive database or resources are scattered among a number of community agencies, the library has an obligation to try to develop a reliable information source that is user friendly and convenient for its clientele. Today many of these are available in electronic formats, on a database or through a Web site.

The library's collection of parenting materials is an integral part of its information and referral service. The collection should be designed for professionals who work with families as much as for parents themselves. The children's librarian needs to be informed and ready to use the collection when assisting parents, teachers, family support providers, and others working with young children and families.

Building a comprehensive parent/professional information collection and community coilitions has been fully described in *Serving Families and Children through Partnerships* (Feinberg and Feldman 1996). *Including Families and Children with Special Needs* (Feinberg et al. 1998) offers extensive resource listings as well as techniques and strategies on providing information and referral to parents.

# SERVING AS AN INFORMATION PROVIDER FOR PROFESSIONALS

When children's librarians become involved in networking and coalition building, they often find themselves assisting family support professionals with their reference needs. Building a parent/professional resource collection and serving the information needs of family support professionals offer children's librarians another opportunity to broaden the scope of services. The materials incorporated within the parents' collection provide a basic collection for family service professionals as well as a starting point for most reference queries.

In addition to the standard parents' fare, however, a professional may require a more in-depth approach or access to special materials in order to satisfy their information needs. Children's librarians need to become familiar with materials located in the adult services department and be able to examine items available through interlibrary loan or through the Internet. See Chapter 4 for a listing of resources that can help librarians build collections for both parents and professionals.

Some of the specific topics based on a list by Barbara Jordan (1996) that professionals may be interested in pursuing include:

developmentally appropriate environments and activities

parent-teacher communications

early childhood curriculum materials

art and recreational activities

creative movement and music activities

parent education programs and curriculums

resource guides to children's books and related activities

classroom management and discipline techniques

working with pregnant and parenting teens

family centered care

conflict resolution

multicultural education

model family support programs and services

child-care training and administration

working with culturally diverse groups

working with diverse family structures

child abuse and neglect

family dysfunction

The integration of information and resource sharing builds the skills and knowledge of the librarian. Discussing information needs with other professionals often broadens the librarian's knowledge and enhances his or her ability to better serve the parents who come into the library. Resource sharing can be a catalyst for further development of cooperative ventures and often provides the librarian with professional expertise to build the parent/professional collection. This is a prime example of using patron (in this case the professional) input as a resource for collection development.

Parents who contact the library to find activities and programs for their children are a potential audience for other programs and services. Children's programs provide a vehicle to introduce parents to the librarian's information and referral role. While children may be the primary focus for story time or an art or nature program, parents and caregivers are also important.

For many parents, a parenting crisis may be precipitated by typical behavior as well as normally occurring developmental milestones. When this happens, the need to talk to someone is usually very strong. Parents rely on each other for information. They seek out individuals with experience as parents and/or as professionals to provide answers and support. Children's programs often generate a great deal of interest on the part of parents who see these programs as providing a safe opportunity to ask questions regarding development, child rearing, education, and/or family issues. On such occasions, parents are generally receptive to hearing about services that can enhance their ability to be more effective parents.

Although the library has print, video, and electronic resources to address the questions, the key to successful communication with parents is being familiar with local service providers. High-quality information and referral is based on current knowledge of local agencies and an understanding of what these agencies can offer. This type of knowledge is critical to the provision of comprehensive parent information services.

Beyond having the information and materials, library staff need to promote the use of library resources including information and referral as an integral part of overall community service. Staff must be able and prepared for readers' (and viewers') advisory, to recommend the appropriate books, videos, electronic resources, and community services to meet the information and learning needs of families with young children. While all this may seem to be a great deal of responsibility for a library to take on, it can be done effectively with the cooperation of other community agencies.

There is a logical continuum of involvement with community organizations, beginning with making connections to other groups that serve parents. By letting parent education services know what the library has to offer regarding information, materials and programs for parents, caregivers and young children, the library is, in effect, reaching the clientele of all those agencies and organizations. Though there is no right or wrong way to become linked to community services concerned with the needs and interests of young children and their families, it is important to take that first step and make the commitment to get involved at some level.

## COALITION BUILDING

It is essential that children's librarians forge links within the early childhood and parent education community. In their book, *Serving Families and Children through Partnerships: A How-to-Do-It Manual for Librarians* (1996), Feinberg and Feldman outline four basic models of coalition building. The spectrum of coalition building ranges from networking to establishing collaborations. Coalition building integrates the library with the greater community of early childhood and parenting services and increases the library's potential for reaching families. Other groups benefit through the library's special collections and the librarian's ability to provide information and referral to the community.

Networking is a formal communication model that goes beyond introducing library services to agencies and organizations. Generally it involves people meeting face-to-face on a regular basis to talk about their work with young children and families, provide updates on new programs and services, and exchange brochures, flyers, and newsletters. This personal information exchange assists librarians in their efforts to make effective referrals, build relevant collections, develop programs around pertinent issues, and forge new professional and personal friendships. It reduces the isolation of many professionals who work in small programs, schools, centers, or agencies or who are based in rural or suburban communities.

The next levels of coalition building are coordination and cooperation. These offer different levels of involvement for the library. Coordination enables both the library and an agency to recognize each other's offerings and avoid duplicating services already available. Joint advertising, publicity, marketing, and programming efforts conserve resources while respecting the existing identities and services of each agency.

Cooperation requires a greater level of commitment and usually involves a joint effort such as working closely with another agency, organization, or parent group to sponsor a workshop. A new venture may be established in which both agencies serve families together. A parents' support group in which the agency provides the facilitator and the library provides space and promotional materials is another example of cooperation. Both the agency and the library reach out to their respective clientele for participation.

Coalition building stimulates the creation of effective outreach programs. For example, cooperative efforts have led to a successful program that integrates toddlers with developmental disabilities with typical toddlers at library story time. In this model, an early intervention provider attends the program along with the child. This specialist supports the parents and helps supervise the child during story time. She then introduces related activities or materials to the child between programs. Alternatively, a specialist may offer advice on specific techniques to use in adapting a program or activity for a child with a special need. The library's goal to reach out and include children with special needs is achieved. Simultaneously, the early intervention program fulfills its requirements to make use of typical community resources in the effort to mainstream families.

Partnerships require additional financial and time commitments from the library and other agencies and organizations that join together to address community needs. The financial commitment can involve an in-kind contribution or actual cash. Two or more groups may join together to bring a national speaker to a community, with each group contributing some percentage of the speaker's fee. A family literacy program may use a branch library as an instructional site. The family literacy program provides staff and computers that can be used by families visiting the library. The library provides office space, power for the computers, and use of the community or meeting room on a regular basis. Librarians may also work with the families by providing special story times or workshops on accessing library services.

Collaborations enable new services to be introduced into the community. The library and other groups identify a need and establish a program or project to meet that need. An example might be the establishment of a hands-on children's museum. It could begin as the collaborative brainstorm of the library, PTO, Child Care Council, and the art museum, all of whom see a need for new cultural and educational enrichment for families in the community. Grant writing could lead to the establishment of a museum corner in the library (or it could be in the art museum or a school). All initial parties make an investment of in-kind or staff resources. The project may either grow or be maintained at the initial level. The most successful collaborations often take on their own identity.

Children's librarians have never been people to stand on ceremony. If you won't come to their "house," they'll come to yours. Visits to day-care centers, Head Start programs, nursery schools, family child-care providers, pediatric clinics, WIC* clinics, immunization programs, zoos, and prenatal programs are standard locations for library programs or off-site collections. The wide range of language-based activities, informational and educational services, and associated library resources including collections are often taken on the road. One goal of these presentations is to introduce library services to non-library users. Another goal is to form a relationship with agency personnel, building connections that can lead to further cooperative efforts and become a vehicle for the library to reach out to new family audiences.

Putting a regular procedure in place to contact potential outreach locations will facilitate the development of a working relationship with a wide variety of community agencies and groups. Contact procedures can range from periodic mailings (low impact) to a regular schedule of phone calls and visits (high impact). Visits are not only high impact in terms of marketing the library's service, but they are also the opportunity for library staff to connect with agency or organization personnel who have a commitment to common goals. The personal connection is important. It leads to the development of trust that can inspire shared creative endeavors from joint programs to joint grant proposals.

In today's early childhood environment, there are many reasons that people can't or won't access libraries. Families may be isolated from the library because of physical distance; inconvenient hours; lack of transportation; inaccessible facilities; or lack of experience and knowledge of library services and programs. Child-care providers may find that the number of children in their care prohibits library use or that liability issues when traveling with young children make visiting the library difficult.

The timing and location of library programs critically influence who can attend. Libraries need to be flexible in their program scheduling if they intend to reach children of working parents. Evening story times, Saturday morning workshops, and after-school programs target those children who cannot come during traditional library programming hours. Allowing nonparental caregivers to bring children to library programs and designing cooperative programs with child-care providers are essential strategies for reaching the children of working families.

The increasing involvement of fathers in library programs is a result of an overall interest in parent education, a steady growth of women in the work force, and the blossoming dual custody arrangements in divorce settlements. Today, many fathers share the responsibility of child raising and child care. They are looking for things to do with their young children. While some fathers are at ease attending a program aimed at mothers and children, this may not be the most effective way

---

*Special Supplemental Food Program for Women, Infants and Children.

to reach the majority of fathers. Designing programs especially for dads that build on male communication and play styles and that address some of their particular concerns and questions should be a service priority.

Promoting the use of the library by families with children who have disabilities and families with young children whose parent has a disability requires a willingness to adapt programs and services to accommodate individual needs, as well as tapping additional outreach strategies. Physical therapists and early intervention professionals are important contacts to reach these populations and to provide training and information to librarians. Special adaptations such as hiring a sign-language interpreter, placing an easily distractible child at the front of the room near the librarian, or investing in Braille and large-print picture books are some examples of adapting services. Incorporating assistive technology in the children's computer area or displaying posters that depict children and/or adults with disabilities advertises to families that the library is an inclusive place.

Adolescent parents require other approaches. Often these parents are without transportation or do not feel welcome in a room full of "right-age" moms and dads. Programs may need to be tailored for this population. Addressing the developmental needs of teenagers while acknowledging their role as parents requires creativity. It is often necessary to work with community agencies that already serve this population in order to reach this audience, increase the staff's sensitivity to their needs, and provide appropriate information resources.

The growing presence of immigrant families in some communities presents a special challenge to libraries. Librarians may need to explain library policies and practices to families who are not fluent in English or who bring conflicting expectations to the library building. Working with agencies that already serve these communities is one step that can enable librarians to learn more about the cultures, focus on the particular issues of importance to the families, and develop ways of assisting families to feel comfortable in the library environment. Preparing flyers or brochures in the home languages represented in the community, having translators available to assist parents in Parent/Child Workshops, and inviting community leaders from diverse ethnic backgrounds to take part in panel presentations, on advisory boards, and in focus groups are the types of strategies that can be employed to help all young families feel welcome in the library.

The outreach program expands the four walls of the library. It is not just a promotional tool for in-house services but an extension of the library facility that improves the library's ability to meet the needs of the community. Though it is impossible to meet the needs of all community groups, programs, and agencies, children's librarians need to target the early childhood and parent education community in order to reach families that are not able to access library services on their own.

Working with agencies and organizations will result in logical models and extensions of library service. One example could be offering story hour in a neighborhood church or other community center so that nearby family child-care providers can walk children there to participate in the program. Another extension of library services might involve providing additional evening story times in a community where the majority of families have two working parents. Packaging materials in a book bag or kit specifically designed for family home day-care providers and after-school programs is another alternative to traditional library service. Rotating books for young children through neighborhood retail establishments where young children spend waiting hours—places like laundromats, automobile service stations, or medical clinics—may be another opportunity to reach emergent readers in community outposts.

# INTERDISCIPLINARY TRAINING AND PROFESSIONAL INVOLVEMENT

Perhaps the important professional outreach role for the children's librarian becomes one of instruction. This involves developing and updating bibliographies of developmentally appropriate materials and informing other professionals about the importance of play, reading, and book sharing for language development. It may be more beneficial for library staff to provide in-service training programs for day-care, nursery school, and Head Start teachers than to visit a multitude of sites on a regular basis. For example, clinic workers with in-service training on the importance of reading aloud to children beginning at birth are better able to provide instruction to parents during prenatal classes and well-child checkups. Picture book bibliographies, pamphlets on reading to infants and toddlers, and flyers on library services for families and young children can be distributed through these programs.

Children's librarians can, in turn, look to other agencies and organizations to provide in-service training to library staff. Preparing to work with parents and children with a wide range of developmental disabilities requires an understanding of the disabilities. It may also require learning effective communication techniques. Many agencies will provide training to staff or have an expert on staff who can be called upon for advice. Sharing knowledge and expertise is a result of better communication and networking.

Professionals from other agencies are often willing to meet with and train parents in the library setting. The library as a nonjudgmental and information-oriented community meeting place strikes a positive note for most professionals who need to see parents. The professional may see the librarian as a natural ally in an effort to reach families. This can result in a team teaching activity on the part of both agencies involved and is a primary example of cooperative programming.

Librarians must advocate for coalition building within the library and related early childhood professional associations. Professionals must seek their own level of involvement within local, state, and national library associations. It is essential that children's librarians have a voice in those organizations and also bring the knowledge and experience of the early childhood community to bear on the policy and direction of library associations.

Children's librarians should consider joining other relevant local, state, and national associations. The Family Resource Coalition of America, International Reading Association, and National Association for the Education of Young Children are examples of associations that have local chapters. This is another way to begin the networking process, acquire valuable in-service training, and make an impact on the library's role in early childhood education and services.

Analyzing the librarian's place in the early childhood and family service community may help to define one's own need for training. With increased training comes increased confidence in one's abilities and skills.

# ASSESSMENT OF COLLABORATIONS AND NETWORKS

A belief in and a vision of what the public library has to offer families, children, and agencies in the community should also influence the decision to take a more active role in the community. Although it is not necessary for every library and every children's librarian to be involved in all levels of networking and coalition building, it is essential that the children's librarian have firsthand knowledge of and be a player in early childhood and family support communities.

Reviewing the library's efforts to build collaborative services and provide effective outreach requires that librarians examine documentation of the activities staff members are involved in, the types of cooperative programs and services that are provided, and initiatives in which the library may be involved as a partner. Additional information can be found by interviewing professionals in the community. Specific tools that apply to the review of collaborations and networks include B-2, B-3, B-6, B-7, D-5, D-6, D-7, and D-8.

REFERENCES

*The family place: A prospectus.* 1997. New York: Libraries for the Future.

Feinberg, S., et al. 1998. *Including families and children with special needs.* New York: Neal-Schuman.

Feinberg, S., and S. Feldman. 1996. *Serving families and children through partnerships.* New York: Neal-Schuman.

Jordan, B. 1996. Building a family support collection. Chap. 11 in *Serving families and children through partnerships,* by S. Feinberg and S. Feldman. New York: Neal-Schuman.

# 6

# Administration

Children's services are an integral part of a library's program. In fact some might say that children's services keep public libraries vibrant, energetic, and at the cutting edge of education, recreation, and information. Most communities are supportive of environments and activities that encourage a positive use of leisure time and support services to young children within the library's mission.

The library offers a place and program for families of all economic and social levels. Often referred to as a community center or town hall, it can serve as a central meeting place. The opportunity for social interaction across cultural and economic lines may be one of the most powerful elements of public library service today and into the twenty-first century. Nurtured properly, it can have a profound impact on a young child's sense of community.

Pulling back from the projected vision and image of children's services in public libraries, it is necessary to examine the internal dynamics that determine whether a program thrives or barely survives. What is the place of the children's librarian(s) in the library's internal hierarchy? How do other staff members interact with and involve the children's librarian(s) in planning and service development? How are budgets created and appropriated within the library? Are children's services "separate but equal" or integrated and equal?

Children's librarians need to assess the library's overall services for young children and families, taking a broad look at the range of offerings and how they are developed and promoted. They need to manage the daily tasks and work priorities of their staff, realign resources, and examine internal practices and procedures. Redesigning programs and collections to reflect child development and family needs not only advances the perception and image of the children's department but systemically changes the direction and focus of the library's role in the community. Serving parents and adults who work with families advances the level of service which in turn garners respect for the role of children's librarians.

# STRATEGIC PLANNING

Holly G. Willett in *Public Library Youth Services* (1995) provides a comprehensive overview and a series of recommendations that could effectively change the image and impact of youth services. Recommendation 14 states "[Y]outh services librarians must be able to market their services with research and theoretical background demonstrating the educational and economic value of public library services to young people. Further, youth services librarians must study the education, economics, and demographics of their particular communities in order to show the library director, the library board of trustees, the public and the local government how their services fit not just the national or state pictures but also the local one." (235)

Willett understands the competitive environment of libraries and library funding. In order for children's services to be successful, librarians must understand the environment and the politics of their community. The process always begins with a detailed environmental analysis that provides quantitative and qualitative data. Most of these data may be already available in the library, other community agencies, or government offices. Schools and other community agencies such as Head Start and child care councils conduct periodic needs assessments that include a critical look at the community. Such needs assessments typically analyze the community and suggest priorities in service to families and children. The library may have already accessed appropriate demographics and family profiles as part of a larger planning process.

The environmental analysis provides an overview of the whole community of early childhood services. Knowing key players and their priorities can help to identify and focus the library's role. The other agencies and organizations committed to early childhood programs are natural allies and partners for developing new projects, advocating for legislation and enhancing existing services. See chapter 5 for a detailed look at partnerships and collaborations.

Information gathering and utilization are a librarian's forte. A detailed understanding of the community is the key for designing an effective strategic plan for the library's service for children and families; setting appropriate missions, goals, and objectives; developing activities, collections, and programs; and expanding services based on ongoing evaluation and assessment. The plan is not a fixed blueprint but a map to guide the staff toward better practice. Short-term and long-term objectives need to be fluid within this plan, recognizing that there are many alternative routes for achieving similar outcomes. The staff must work together with families and early childhood service providers to weigh options, focus on community segments, and prioritize services. Surveys, focus groups, and interviews may be conducted regularly to help steer the course of program initiatives. Information gathering is an ongoing process.

The plan for children's services does not occur in a vacuum. The library's children's services are part of the greater community and part of the total library program. An effective plan must be coordinated with the library's strategic or long-range plan. The library board, director, and other staff must support the objectives, outcomes, and activities to ensure success. The best process involves these players at the outset. Just as the target audience must feel ownership in the program, so must colleagues and administrators.

# POLICIES AND PROCEDURES

Library policies create the potential for successful early childhood and family centered services. Policies that are family centered encourage participation by even the youngest members of the community and welcome parents and caregivers. Policies that limit access and rights for children are barriers to effective involvement. In today's environment, some parents may encourage libraries to adopt special borrowing and usage policies in place of free access to information and services for minors. This negative approach to library service for children is usually born of fear and misunderstanding. By educating and informing parents about the library's role and their own role and responsibility, a better relationship can be established. Potential conflict may be minimized.

Organizational commitment to families is often demonstrated by the policy language in library documents and communication tools that are used to inform the community about library policy. Children's librarians should be proactive in developing and reviewing library policies, procedures, and communications that may impact families' and children's use of the library to its fullest. One first step is calling attention to family or children's issues that are overlooked by individuals whose primary foci are adult patrons. Working with the administration, children's librarians need to initiate new policies or policy changes when necessary. Support from the administration on policy is support for the entire children's services program.

The children's librarian cannot expect support unless policies are carefully planned, the community's attitude and experience are considered, and the children's staff has done a good job of preparing and presenting policy recommendations to the director. Emotional or flippant approaches, without considering all implications and outcomes, will not be welcomed. Having too casual an attitude about policy and procedure can result in being "locked out" of the director's advisory group. The director and other administrators do not want to be embarrassed or receive community complaints because of a thoughtless change in policy or the initiation of an unwelcome procedure.

Some areas that need clear policy formation include:

library card registration—particularly age of eligibility, responsibility, and parent or caregiver involvement
confidentiality

free access to information for minors

use of technology and Internet access

community access to meeting rooms, bulletin boards, or display areas

fines and fees

access to equipment

circulation—particularly the issues of renewals, reserves, interlibrary loans, and nonbook materials

reference and program services—including homework assistance, telephone reference responses, and registration procedures

photocopying

unattended children

behavior standards and limits

hours of service

cleanliness and safety

When examining policies and procedures, it is often recommended that the library involve the staff and the public. A resource that helps children's librarians select and analyze library policies is *Kids Welcome Here! Writing Public Library Policies That Promote Use by Young People* (1990). Focus groups, surveys, and interviews may also give librarians the information necessary to change a policy or precedent. Long-term policies may need to be carefully reviewed.

One example involves library card registration. Many libraries require children to sign their name before getting a library card. This sends a mixed message for those who want to encourage parents to use libraries for children beginning at birth. In fact, writing one's name has no relevance for borrowing books and materials or using the library. An adult who is illiterate or a preschooler who can already read but cannot write are both appropriate library borrowers. If the library has strict registration policies, the children's librarian needs to do some homework. Does the director agree with this policy or is it an old policy that can be modified? Interview staff of neighboring libraries. Their policies may be less restrictive. Talk with parents who have young children. Maybe they would approach the director or write letters or complete suggestion forms that advocate a change in the policy.

Another critical and current issue is use of technology and access to the Internet. Children's librarians need to participate actively in decision making on all policies and procedures regarding technology. Questions and concerns include: Do young children have access to a full range of new technologies? Are parents encouraged to use technology with their children? Are policies about free access updated to include the Internet or has a separate Internet policy been developed for minors? Are computers provided in the children's room? If not, can children freely access the equipment no matter where it is located in the library? Are there age restrictions on the use of equipment?

It is difficult to change policy, procedure, and precedent. Building evidence and support through community and patron involvement is an effective tool when making a presentation designed to effect change. Handling such a presentation in a professional manner will have an impact on the way a director or board receives the information. Follow-up evaluations and analysis on the impact of a policy or procedural change will make subsequent changes easier to accomplish. Procedure and protocol is usually determined by staff with the approval of the library director. All policies should have the full approval of the board of trustees.

# RESOURCE ALLOCATION

There is probably no better way for the administration and the library director to show their full support for children's services than through the budgetary process. The children's services budget should achieve a percentage match to its percentage of usage by the community. That is to say, if 50 percent of a library's usage is children's services then 50 percent of the budget for department staff, materials, and equipment should be applied to children's services. While this is rarely the case, it is important that the budget move toward "equalizing the wealth" among children's services and other departments, financially supporting the needs of the community. Resource allocation is usually determined by a library's mission, goals, and roles. The children's services department can easily assess the director's commitment by the dollar commitment to the program (Chelton 1997).

Children's librarians should regularly examine output measures and usage in order to move toward equalization. Presenting this information to the director in a professional manner is imperative in order to garner support. Departmental goals need to be based on real figures and determined need. Distributing articles on the importance of children's services, gathering outside community and patron support through letters and word-of-mouth, publishing articles in local newspapers or even professional publications, and making public presentations are some of the effective tools for promoting the value of children's services. Making the library's children's services a visible part of the library on a local, regional, and national level can have an impact on the budgetary process.

Understanding resource allocation at the department level is equally critical. In addition to assessing the availability and distribution of library resources to the entire department, children's librarians need to determine where service for *young* children and families fits in the overall organization and mission of the library. In many instances, librarians may find little in the way of extra library resources available to them. However, a commitment and willingness to change can be key to improvement, even in the face of fiscal limitations. Successful strategies for improving the library's work with young children can run the gamut from revising internal practices and procedures to rethinking the current budget so that resources can be allocated to augment services or collections for young children and their families. Developing cooperative services with other agencies is an additional approach to building support for the library's work with young children and their families.

The director can be a forceful ally in rallying corporate, government, and private financial support for the children's program. Funding for children is often an attractive venture for outside groups. Directors can help the children's department build bridges to other organizations and networks throughout the community. Collaborative grants cannot usually be completed without the agreement of the director. His or her support and encouragement is critical to success.

## CLEANLINESS AND SAFETY

The administration needs to be concerned about cleanliness and safety as programs for young children and families bring this audience to the library. Space, furniture, bathrooms, and waste disposal all present hazards to young, mobile children using the facility. On the flip side, having family space, furniture, and convenient rest rooms are all part of the program design and demonstrate administrative support for early childhood services.

Involving the children's services librarian in facility planning, in meetings with cleaning staff and custodial services, and on the library's safety committees is essential. Chapter 3 provides detailed information on the physical environment for young children including safety issues that need to be addressed.

## PROGRAM AND SERVICE DEVELOPMENT

Librarians need to look at the overall program, collection, and service offerings including the full spectrum of services available in relationship to the targeted audiences. They need to consider their relationship to family literacy and lifelong learning. Other considerations include the breadth and depth of library service for young children and families, scheduling and staffing for effective program delivery, audience range, managing and administering available resources, and ongoing assessment of services to measure impact.

## A Continuum of Service

The administration of the library needs to accept the mandate to offer a continuum of service for young children and their families. A regular pattern of library use for families often begins with the birth of a child. A seamless sequence of services should be available from that first connection.

There is an array of replicable library-based and library-promoted early childhood models available. The early childhood profession has identified this period as encompassing the years from birth through age eight. Story times for toddlers, preschoolers, and primary grade children, the Parent/Child Workshop, Mother Goose programs and family reading clubs are already standard fare in many libraries that provide services for young children. Library service delivery could also begin with contacting new parents or making visits to local hospitals.

Connecting families with books during these earliest days not only encourages families to read together during the early years but also identifies the library as a key community resource.

## The Art of Scheduling and Staffing

Staff scheduling for early childhood and family centered services involves simultaneously orchestrating the services of library professionals and support staff within programs, at the children's reference desk, and in the children's area. Organizational issues include the distribution of program assignments, the allotment of preparation time, the spacing of programs throughout the day, and inherent variations in required setup and cleanup time. An integrated schedule is one that reflects the entire range of program offerings and reference desk coverage. It helps avoid conflicts, keeps the department on track, and provides a "quick check" when assessing overall department offerings.

Many libraries use volunteers or train staff to work in all areas of the library. Creative and flexible contingency planning has to be worked into staffing considerations. Competent scheduling and support for programming are necessary regardless of staffing configurations.

## The Registration Process

An effective way to ascertain staff requirements and to understand patrons' programmatic preferences is to analyze program registration. Preregistration allows librarians to determine the level of interest, control the number in attendance, and become familiar with the names of participants. Program popularity can be a guide for developing future offerings. The feasibility of opening additional sessions to accommodate people on waiting lists or families who wish to repeat a program can also be evaluated in conjunction with registration information.

The registration process itself is not always favored by patrons, particularly those interested in popular programs. Complaints about the registration procedure were often voiced during the *Early Childhood Quality Review Initiative* (1995) field testing. As a result, one library changed its program registration procedures. This particular library had required in-person registration to determine eligibility, resulting in long lines on registration day. During the review process, it was suggested that the library use numbered tickets so that parents and children could wait in a separate area rather than standing in line. The availability of toys, puzzles, crafts and even coffee, juice, and cookies in an activity room adjacent to the registration area now makes registration a social event. These changes were designed to make the registration experience as pleasant as possible.

Placing too many children in one program, popular or not, can diminish the positive impact. Too many children reflects poor planning, elicits a negative response from patrons and staff, and is developmentally inappropriate. Overbooking undermines program quality. When there are insufficient resources or staff, the program may have less value for both children and parents. Children cannot readily participate or receive the necessary attention if programs are overcrowded. A poor staff-to-child ratio also affects the ease with which a program can be adapted to the particular needs of children with disabilities.

## Audience Range

Library programs need to target a wide range of participant audiences: parent/caregiver and child together, child only, parent only, children within local preschools and child-care centers, children with family home day-care providers or classmates, parent and/or children with social worker, counselor, or agency representative, multi-age sibling or family groupings. Scheduling issues arise around each of these types of planned programs. Coordination with child-care centers, preschools, Head Start programs, and family day-care homes is essential. It is also critical to schedule evening and Saturday programs for working parents or parents who attend school on weekdays. Knowing the community and how best to reach the maximum number of children, alone and with their parents, is a vital part of schedule and program coordination.

## PROGRAM DEVELOPMENT

When programs are in demand, it is best to discuss the specific needs and resources with the library director or supervisor. This will both alert the administration to the interest in the program or service and provide an opportunity for considering a range of alternative solutions to satisfy demand. Both space and staff issues concern the allocation of resources.

Short-term solutions to high levels of program demand could involve the use of volunteers or the reassignment of staff. Space shortage may require changing the hours of service in the children's department to increase program availability. Long-range planning may suggest the use of other community locations, the hiring of additional staff, or the cultivation of a Friends group to offer additional volunteer and fundraising support.

Administrators, boards, community organizations, and parents need to work with librarians to find solutions to programming needs. Parents of young children are a key library audience and can advocate for children's services. Few libraries want to disappoint this vocal and proactive group of library supporters.

# Goals of Programming

The selection of appropriate books and materials is a critical step to program planning. Books used within the program or that support the theme or topic of the session need to be available in sufficient quantity so that parents and children can take them home after the program. This not only extends learning, but also teaches young children about the process of borrowing materials and what it means to have a library card.

Within library settings, a primary aim of programming is to introduce parents/caregivers to appropriate materials for young children and to demonstrate how to interact with children around these materials. Using puppets and flannelboards, telling stories, and singing songs are entertaining. However, the fundamental goal is to provide activities that will facilitate learning and encourage emergent literacy for young children both within the library setting and at home. Librarians, though often entertaining, are not in the entertainment business.

Creating library patrons who are lifelong learners is a major goal of programming. Program participation stimulates interest in materials among children and parents. Multiple copies of books used in programs, handouts with the words of the nursery rhymes or songs sung as part of a program, and bibliographies of related materials are necessary "tools of the trade" when working with young children and their families. Displaying related books and materials expands ideas presented in the program. When preparing programs for young children, it is often helpful to have these selected items for circulation readily available in the programming room. This accommodates the tired child and guides parents on appropriate materials to use at home.

# COLLECTION DEVELOPMENT

Principles of collection development combined with theories of developmentally appropriate practice, family centered service, family literacy, and family information literacy inform effective and valuable collections that serve children and families. Selection and acquisition policies and practices must ensure availability of pertinent materials for both children and parents. Staff needs to order materials on a planned and orderly basis, keeping in mind the scope and breadth of the collections. Materials must reflect and promote awareness of diversity of age, ability, gender, experience, language, and cultural backgrounds. Patron input is a must.

## Circulating Materials

Librarians must actively search for and promote picture books that span the early childhood years, beginning with infancy. In addition to books, toys, puzzles, videos, board and cloth books, compact discs, CD-ROM software, and audiocassettes are relevant circulating materials appropriate for very young children. Many of the resources listed later in this chapter include bibliographic and processing information on books, audiovisuals, and toys. Collections are further discussed in chapters 3, 4, and 5.

Encouraging parents to use library materials at home is a primary job of the children's librarian. Having an ample supply of popular materials, generous circulation and reserve policies, special exhibits and displays, and easily accessible materials provides the flexibility librarians need to accomplish this goal.

Resources encompass not only collections for children but for parents and adults who work with families and children. Chapters on parent participation and collaborations and networks discuss these collections in greater detail. However, it is important that children's librarians review their offerings to determine the depth and scope of the parent/professional collection, the range and types of materials and the resources allocated to support this collection relative to the entire book collection.

## In-House Collections

Collections for use in the library setting are effective if organized to attract the interests of young children and promote accessibility and independence. Librarians need to create a stimulus-rich environment for young children that integrates appropriate materials including books, art supplies, manipulative and building materials, and some form of equipment and materials for music and pretend play. Materials should be readily available to satisfy program needs and drop-in use. Each library must assess its own requirements based on space, programming, and budget. Chapter 3 describes procedures for creating or evaluating a suitable early childhood space within the library.

## Parent/Professional Collection

This collection for parents and adults who work with families needs to be accessible within or adjacent to the children's room. Children's librarians need to familiarize themselves with these materials along with reference materials, periodicals, and electronic resources aimed at parents and family support professionals. Providing bibliographies of both children's materials and family-focused resources can aid adults in the selection process.

# Computer Technology

Access to new technologies and electronic resources is vital for young children and families. Helping children as well as their parents use computers is a critical role for the children's librarian and facilitates family computer literacy. Computer skills include but are not limited to discovery learning and problem solving, use of graphics, word processing, and accessing information. Providing computer keyboards and computer software designed with young children in mind should be at the forefront of current collection development initiatives. Involving parents with their child's use of and access to Internet resources can reduce fears or concerns about access to inappropriate Web sites.

## CHILDREN'S PROGRAMS AND COLLECTIONS
### Selected Resources

Briggs, D. 1993. *Toddler storytime programs.* School Library Media Series. No. 2. Metuchen, N.J.: Scarecrow.

Carlson, A. D. 1985. *Early childhood literature sharing programs in libraries.* Hamden, Conn.: Library Professional Publications.

DeSalvo, N. N. 1993. *Beginning with books: Library programming for infants, toddlers and preschoolers.* Hamden, Conn.: Library Professional Publications.

Dowd, F. S., and J. Dixon. 1996. Successful toddler storytimes based on child development principles. *Public Libraries* (November/December): 374–80.

Ernst, L. L. 1995. *Lapsit: Programming for the very young.* New York: Neal-Schuman.

Feinberg, S., and K. Deerr. 1995. *Running a parent/child workshop: A how-to-do-it manual for librarians.* New York: Neal-Schuman.

Feinberg, S., and S. Feldman. 1996. *Serving families and children through partnerships: A how-to-do-it manual for librarians.* New York: Neal Schuman.

Feinberg, S. et al. 1998. *Including families and children with special needs: A how-to-do-it manual for librarians.* New York: Neal-Schuman.

Greene, E. 1991. *Books, babies, and libraries: Serving infants, toddlers, their parents, and caregivers.* Chicago: American Library Association.

Herb, S., and S. Willoughby-Herb. 1994. *Using children's books in preschool settings: A how-to-do-it manual.* New York: Neal-Schuman.

Jacobson, J. R. 1994. Ready to read. *Baby Talk* (August): 32–35.

Jeffery, D. A. 1995. *Literate beginnings: Programs for babies and toddlers.* Chicago: American Library Association.

Lamme, L. L., and A. B. Packer. 1986. Bookreading behaviors of infants. *The Reading Teacher* (February): 504–9.

Marino, J., and D. Houlihan. 1992. *Mother Goose time: Library programs for babies and their caregivers.* New York: Wilson.

Nespeca, S. M. 1994. *Library programming for families with young children: A how-to-do-it manual for librarians.* New York: Neal-Schuman.

*Partners for inclusion: Welcoming infants and toddlers with disabilities and their families into community activities: A resource guide.* 1997. Hauppauge, N.Y.: Suffolk County Department of Health Services.

*Programming for serving children with special needs.* 1994. Chicago: American Library Association.

Rogers, P., and B. Herrin. 1986. Parent-child learning centers: An alternative approach to library programming for preschoolers. *Top of the News* (summer): 343–55.

# MARKETING

Any library marketing program should have children's services as the centerpiece of its promotional campaign. Service to children and parents is easily defined and the audience is easy to target. Others in the community will have a positive impression of a library that considers the needs and interests of families and young children.

Community concerns and solutions to social issues can become marketing advantages for the children's services department. The middle class, a traditional audience for libraries, will openly receive the message that "reading begins at birth." The positive approach to education, community networks, and a welcoming environment is a plus for reaching the disadvantaged and discouraged.

Many successful children's programs, recognized by parents, children, and the community as satisfying a basic need for learning and connecting with others, fulfill a fundamental role of the public library. Early childhood services have a particular appeal because there are few publicly funded institutions that have laid claim to this territory and that offer programs across socioeconomic lines. This is a wonderful opportunity for libraries.

## Customer Service

Looking at it through the eyes of an administrator, programming in the children's department is an excellent customer service strategy. It provides an ongoing method for communicating with families, one of the library's most important advocate groups. It builds relationships with parents and initiates an early pattern of library use that, ideally, will be repeated when the children themselves become parents.

Word of mouth is the library's most powerful public relations tool. This tool relies on good customer service and the staff's efforts to pay attention to the needs and desires of patrons. Good customer service spreads positive messages about the library's services and often brings hesitant and new patrons into the library.

## Advertising and Promotion

How the library advertises its programs and services for young children is critical to their success. All library programs need to be promoted at the library and through typical promotional vehicles such as newsletters, news releases, and flyers. Contacts should be made with child-care centers and child-care councils, preschools, grandparent support groups, and other social service organizations to facilitate the inclusion of library program announcements in their in-house newsletters or circulars. Distributing flyers and program notices in places frequented by parents, such as laundromats, grocery stores, and pediatricians' offices, can be effective.

# Media Relationships

Media relationships must be established and nurtured. Developing positive media relationships can mean feature stories on library events, an ongoing column by a librarian or staff member, or a personal contact when filler photos or news pieces are needed by print, radio, or television journalists. Positive press can recruit new users to the library. Courting reporters from print and electronic media can be essential to the promotion of the program within the greater community and within the library itself. A continuous positive drumbeat to the administration that underscores the importance of children's services to the community can result in sustained funding, board and administrative commitment, and the expansion of the children's and family services departments. Children's staff should not rely on a public relations director or another staff person to generate the interest and the press releases. This is an area where personally taking charge will result in the greatest visibility.

# ONGOING EVALUATION AND ASSESSMENT

Ongoing evaluation of services and programs is essential. Statistics regarding circulation and in-house use of children's and parents' materials provide proof to administrators of the popularity of and demand for a particular collection or service. Waiting lists inform the staff when additional program sessions are needed. They may be used, along with attendance and registration records, as both a source of information about current community interests and a list of potential library advocates and/or parent advisors.

Other forms of data may be used in conjunction with waiting lists to determine whether or not to continue or expand a particular program. Assessment informs library practice for both the librarian and the parent. However, evaluation must take into account the many ways children and adults learn, as well as the diversity of their experience, language, and cultural backgrounds. Both an evaluation form for parents and an end-of-session wrap-up with staff help provide better service to the community.

Staff needs to be directly involved in all decisions affecting programs and they need information to make these decisions. This may involve "fine-tuning" or refining programs that are well received while eliminating, rescheduling, or revamping others. All of the librarians who participated in the *Early Childhood Quality Review Initiative* acknowledged a lack of program evaluation tools. After the review experience, they felt strongly that the review process provides a method for improving the program content and service offerings.

Planning documentation provides a road map for staff, outlining specific objectives and goals associated with each service. An annual assessment to discuss strengths and weaknesses of overall service offerings and to plan for the next year's service goals allows staff to reflect on where they are going and what they are trying to accomplish. Parent surveys can inform librarians about children's learning experiences at the library and the perception of families. One review team member who participated in the *Early Childhood Quality Review Initiative* found that parents recognize repeated requests for reading particular stories at home as a direct outcome of visiting the library.

# ASSESSMENT OF ADMINISTRATION

Oftentimes, when librarians step back to review the library's service for young children and families they see unlimited opportunities with limited resources. Understanding what is possible, taking small steps to enhance and modify services, and advocating for the realignment of resources are part of the process. These ongoing efforts will enable librarians and libraries to offer a wider range of service to the community and take a leadership role in serving young children and families.

When considering the administrative issues surrounding library-based early childhood services, librarians must take into consideration the overall administrative policies and procedures as well as their own efforts at managing a department. Looking at the distribution of resources within the library, examining policies that affect service to children, involving oneself in the overall marketing and strategic planning of the administration, and developing and managing children's programs and collections affect the quality of service provided to families. Specific tools that apply to administration include forms A-1 to A-7, B-1, B-2, B-3, B-5, B-7, B-8, B-9, B-10, B-12, C-6, D-1, D-2, D-3, D-4, D-6, D-7, D-8, and D-9.

REFERENCES

Chelton, M. K. 1997. Three in five public library users are youth. *Public Libraries* 36, no. 2 (March/April): 104–8.

*The Early Childhood Quality Review Initiative for public libraries.* 1995. Centereach, N.Y.: Middle Country Public Library.

*Kids welcome here! Writing public library policies that promote use by young people.* 1990. Ed. A. E. Simon. New York: Youth Services Section, New York Library Association.

Willett, H. G. 1995. *Public library youth services: A public policy approach.* Greenwich, Conn.: Ablex.

# 7

# Professional Development

The job of a children's librarian is very complex and often isolated by the physical environment and the nature of the work. Children's librarians have a wide and varied set of responsibilities that require strong communication skills with a diverse age group, knowledge of and ability to refer patrons to community services, the creation and implementation of regular programs, presentations, and collections, and the effective integration of technology. Their patron base includes not only children from birth but parents, caregivers, and other adults who work with and for families. The scope of the job seems to be growing exponentially as libraries extend elements of instruction, assessment, community outreach, user involvement, and planning into all aspects of children's services.

Irrespective of whether she or he is a direct service provider, the manager of a large children's department or, a generalist who has been assigned responsibility for children's services, the children's librarian must be the embodiment of a family centered role model. The contradictions exhibited by a librarian who requests a family centered behavior policy, yet cringes at the noise level of five healthy toddlers or the "messy clutter" in a parent-child play area, send a negative message to the rest of the staff and the administration about children and the way they use libraries.

## RECOGNIZING LEARNING IN LIBRARIES

Interactions among a librarian, a child, and the family offer powerful models of facilitated learning. These interactions may be observed in many locations throughout the library and in many forms. Seen through this lens, the reference process with a child or parent stands out as a

**83**

classic example of scaffolding in the zone of proximal development. Preschool story time can be acknowledged as a setting for whole language learning and the development of pre-reading skills. Mother Goose programs for infants and parent-child programs for toddlers can be recognized as opportunities for co-construction of knowledge.

Librarians are most readily recognized for their support of language acquisition and the development of emergent reading skills. Helping children become accustomed to the sound and organization of language prior to the development of actual reading skills is critical to learning. Enjoying words, expanding vocabulary, developing a sense of story line and character, learning to appreciate books, establishing routines and habits around reading and learning, and associating pleasure with reading and books are results of library use by young children. Librarians model for parents the importance of individualizing experience and creating varied opportunities for learning. Building research skills, developing competency with technology, fostering creativity, encouraging decision making, and broadening access for social learning are all part of the librarian's role as educator (see p. 85).

Librarians who work with young children recognize the importance of caring about children's feelings and nurturing their curiosity. A child's sense of security within the library setting, feelings of competence at learning new skills, and excitement in discovering new ideas and information provide a foundation and context for other forms of learning including "learning-to-learn" (Burton White, cited in Gestwicki 1995, p. 235).

## The Librarian as Resource Person

Selecting and arranging materials are a major task of the librarian as a resource person. Understanding that young children learn through the use of an array of manipulative, auditory, and visual materials guides librarians to incorporate play collections such as puzzles, dolls, puppets, art supplies, board and cloth books, as well as music and electronic resources, into the children's room and program environments. While maintaining order and safety, librarians act as consultants on the appropriate selection and use of these materials. They remain available to offer suggestions and assistance; to listen, to observe, and to interact with children; and to model for parents alternative ways of playing with and using resources.

Interacting with the parent and child at the reference desk or when moving around the room, the librarian offers the services of a resource professional, providing access to learning tools and offering assistance on how to use them. In the reference area, librarians respond effectively to inquiries, respecting the individual child's "need to know" and acknowledging the validity of questions. Providing appropriate materials and encouraging their use, whether in a program or within the library setting, exemplifies both consultant and teacher roles.

# A PICTURE OF LEARNING IN LIBRARIES

## Scaffolding skill development

reference interview

discussion in story time

child's independent access to resources

sequential story time programming

child-size furniture

attention-span building

limit setting

## Validating self-motivated learning

introducing a range of resources

modeling for parents

working directly with the child

responding to the child's needs

providing parents with information about developmental issues

acknowledging child's actions and interests

## Encouraging intellectual risk taklng

introducing new resources

issuing library card

offering materials not available at home

providing art and science activities for young children

displaying and integrating culturally diverse resources

nurturing a warm atmosphere

supporting a nonjudgmental environment

## Guiding exploration

program organization and management

layout of the library

reference and readers' advisory

independent access for children

extensive and diverse collections

age-appropriate software

interactive and interage learning opportunities

intergenerational programs

interdisciplinary approaches

resource centers

## Providing terms for concepts and names for feelings

using and sharing literature

creating language-oriented activities and programs

labeling and organizing collections

developing collections that deal with emotional issues and family crises

including children with special needs

demonstrating acceptance of diversity

using gender-free language, illustrations, and displays

## Creating opportunities for discovery and creativity

hands-on activities

special displays or learner centers

developmentally and educationally appropriate programs

access to age-appropriate technology

material rich environment

multicultural exhibits, displays, and collections

planned and safe environment

## Fostering emergent literacy

modeling reading and interest in books

offering opportunities for listening and following directions

introducing new vocabulary

encouraging remembering

sharing experiences

playing with language

guiding children to understand story lines

identifying characters

enhancing concept development

integrating ideas and experience

enjoying and showing interest in books

comparing word sounds and meanings

introducing numbers and letters

providing information on language and emergent literacy

## Problem solving and suggesting alternative approaches

active listening

conflict resolution

choice of materials

educational software

Web searches

reference and readers' advisory

community referrals

interloans

parent education materials and programs

handouts for parents

## Creating varied opportunities to communicate

singing for and with children

talking and listening

modeling conflict-resolution strategies

reading interactive stories

demonstrating fingerplays

using manipulatives

introducing puppets

encouraging early peer social interaction

conducting reference interviews

providing summer reading programs

offering parent-child programs

developing interage programming

offering introductions to community networks

supporting parent-to-parent interactions

developing parent/professional partnerships

## Building self-esteem

giving kudos and warm fuzzies

acknowledging child to parent

displaying child's work

rewarding effort

recognizing individual achievement

encouraging questions

The librarian as a resource person or consultant remains "on call" at all times, especially before, during, or after a program. During a program, individual questions are answered within the context of the learning exercise. Before and after a program, the librarian is available for one-on-one interaction.

## The Librarian as Program Presenter

Planning is most critical for the librarian as a facilitator of learning. Designing public programs is no easy task. The younger the patron, the more librarians need to be familiar with growth and development issues in order to be effective in their roles. For young children, activities need to be individualized and child centered. The younger the child the less structured the program format and the more the necessity to focus on offering choices for one-on-one activities. Multiple activity areas and materials need to be incorporated within any program for infants and toddlers.

Infant and toddler programs require that a parent/caregiver be available for individualized attention to each participating child. Introducing infants and toddlers to stories and supporting language acquisition and development requires flexibility and a dependence on the parent/caregiver's interactive assistance. When it is recognized that the ultimate program goals are to encourage parent-child interaction, parent facilitation of emergent literacy, and language enrichment at home, rather than to entertain a group of toddlers in the library, then the need for the significant presence of the parents during infant and toddler programs becomes clear. The librarian needs to remain in the resource role, helping individual parents and toddlers use the materials. Providing follow-up resources such as rhyme and song sheets, bibliographies, parent education materials, or copies of books to take home encourages parents to respect both their child's and their own discoveries.

The preschool child is ready for more group activity and may be able to separate from his or her parent. Librarians assist young children in making the transition to school by offering story time and art or science activity programs that combine group activities with opportunities for individual choices. Continued interaction between the librarian and the child may facilitate the formation of a personal relationship that opens the door to increased opportunities for individualized guided learning.

## The Librarian's Relationship to Administration

An effective relationship with the administration and director means the ongoing opportunity for innovation, change, and the implementation of better practice. Successful collaboration between the director and the children's librarian can lead to more family centered programs not only within the children's department but within other departments or areas of the library as well. Intergenerational, interdepartmental, and outreach services are greatly influenced by the administration's attitude toward children's services.

Children's librarians need to have time away from public service programs and the reference desk. Being able to communicate with colleagues as well as interdepartmentally enables the children's librarian to provide well managed, quality services. Administrative support that allows children's librarians to schedule time for meetings, program planning, administrative tasks, and networking helps set the appropriate tone for the delivery of effective service to the public.

Detailing the individual responsibilities of children's services staff provides children's librarians and administrators with important information about the library's respect and support for children's services. The creation and review of job descriptions and professional planning provide guidance to staff and information to the administration and board. Examining the staff ratio, comparing children's staff to total library staff, and measuring how much staff time is devoted to services designed specifically for young children and parents are objective ways to look at the current level of support.

# STAFF EDUCATION AND TRAINING
## Professional Qualifications

When administration truly values children's services, they find it essential to have qualified specialists provide the service. Hiring MLS librarians with a background in children's services may be a financial hardship for many small libraries. However, the professional training and background of the children's specialist are key to initiating, maintaining, and managing high-quality children's services. Materials selection, program and activity planning, reference service, and overall development of an appropriate environment require a children's library professional. Although one librarian/specialist may be inadequate to meet the needs of the entire community, that person can develop a management plan to involve volunteers and support staff in ways that will ensure a well-rounded program.

The level of staff education and training is an important determinant of the quality of early childhood programs. Working with infants, toddlers, and young children requires unique skill sets that are complementary to but different from those generally needed to work with the older elementary school child. Working with groups of young children in public settings also requires interactive skills that go beyond those required to care for one's own children. Research at child-care centers documents that staff education in early childhood development and/or training in early childhood education is closely associated with positive outcomes for children including increased social interaction with adults, development of prosocial behaviors, and improved language and cognitive development.

Resumes and professional evaluations can be used as a starting point from which to create an overview of the current skills, interests, and qualifications of individuals within a library department. Once these are assessed, in-service training, cross training, and access to professional journals and materials can effectively make use of the background and talents of existing library staff.

## Continuing Education and Training

A proactive approach to program development goes hand-in-hand with staff development. Even if staff members are interested in expanding services, they may not have the background in early childhood education or parent education in order to meet this challenge. Continuous learning among professional and paraprofessional staff is essential. Quality service means ongoing training in areas such as:

children's social, emotional, and physical development
early language learning and development
preschool programming and services
program planning and development
interagency cooperation
communication skills with parents
guiding behavior of young children
social and health issues of families
collection development for the early childhood years, for
      parents, and for professionals working with families
supporting anti-bias programs and environments
identification and reporting of child abuse and neglect
inclusion of children with special needs

Since early childhood and family support services are expanding and developing in the public library field, there is a need for ongoing staff education and training. The amount and kind of necessary educational experience may vary depending on the needs of the program and the particular skills needed by individual staff members. It is important to recognize that even if administrative support for training and education is not available, the individual librarian is personally responsible for acquiring the necessary skills for working with young children and their families.

In order to maintain staff morale and enthusiasm, the development of early childhood and family support expertise needs to be recognized throughout the library as a whole. It is important to ensure that the library's youngest patrons have a positive and safe experience within any area of the library. In addition to children's staff, adult librarians and other library staff should be encouraged to acquire the necessary knowledge of child and human development to accomplish this goal. Supportive feedback from supervisory personnel may assist individuals in these positions to expand their own proficiency in working with young children and their families.

## Professional Education

Within the library field, staff qualifications and training in early childhood and parent education need to be examined. Except for an introduction to children's literature, which may include materials for infants and toddlers, most library schools have no courses aimed at developing professionals with the necessary background and skills to serve this target audience.

Coordination with other degree programs, the provision of specialized educational pathways and credentials, and the development of continuing education courses are important to the implementation of services for young children and families. It may be necessary to enroll in courses at a local university, through distance learning or over the Internet. Collaborating with other agencies that have expertise offers valuable opportunities for shared training between agencies. Professional listservs provide yet another means for the librarian to keep up-to-date regarding the information on early childhood and parent education.

## ADVOCATING FOR CHILDREN'S SERVICES

A children's librarian has the responsibility to serve on community boards and boards of state or national associations. Undertaking community leadership involves taking on one other essential role, the role of advocate. By becoming involved outside the library arena, librarians can bring the library's message of support for families and young children to other groups and organizations. They can also sensitize other leaders about the collaborative potential of the library's services for young children and their families. Communicating clearly and knowledgeably, promoting children's services to staff, involving families in planning and development, and bringing a positive image of the library to the community are all part of the advocacy portfolio.

Strong external advocacy can be put to effective use internally when it is brought to the attention of the director, administration, and board. Conference attendance, professional involvement, and active participation on local boards and committees require administrative support. It is important that administrators be educated to the way in which the library is also enriched by the knowledge, background, and community partnerships that other disciplines bring to the table.

Speaking out on behalf of children's services and speaking up for equality in resource allocation involve preparation and documentation. Knowing when to back down and regroup can also be an important strategy for change. In the event that a children's librarian becomes an administrator, director, or board member, it is essential that he or she retain a commitment to quality early childhood services and continue to advocate on behalf of young children and their families.

# NURTURING QUALITY SERVICE

What is quality service for young children in a library setting? Certain values and assumptions, outlined on page 91, underscore the framework for library-based early childhood services and the library's role in the educational life of a community. The notion of "better practice" is tied directly to the values and assumptions of libraries, learning, and community.

"Better practice" provides better service for the end-user, in this case the young child, his or her parent/caregiver, and the family support service providers in the community. It is generally recognized that "better practice":

is individualized, varied, cognitively and developmentally
    appropriate;
provides equitable access to a rich array of resources and
    learning opportunities;
reflects the strengths, interests, diversity and needs of children
    and their family;
fosters continuous individual development and encourages
    creativity, critical thinking, cooperation, and problem-solving
    skills from birth into adulthood;
implements appropriate policies, programs, and services;
involves partnerships with parents, caregivers, and family service
    providers;
is flexible, accessible, and responsive to children and families.

Current literature yields little in the way of data or guidelines to use in pursuit of "better practice" in the library setting. Therefore, it is the responsibility of children's librarians, listening and interacting with their users, to develop a set of standards. According to Lilian Katz's article "Multiple Perspectives on the Quality of Early Childhood Programs" (1997), programs can be assessed using four different perspectives.

A *top-down perspective* looks at program characteristics such as adult/child ratio or staff qualifications, quantity of space, range and availability of equipment, and safety issues. The *bottom-up perspective* depends primarily on how services are viewed through the child's eyes. What does it feel like (from the child's perspective) to participate in a library program or to use the children's room? Using parents to

# LIBRARY-BASED EARLY CHILDHOOD SERVICE
## Values and Assumptions

### Libraries and the Facilitation of Learning

- The public library is a community-based educational setting in which librarians function as educators, guides, coaches, and facilitators of active learning throughout the life cycle.

- All children can learn and are entitled to equitable access to cognitively enriching, socio-emotionally satisfying, and developmentally appropriate resources and learning opportunities.

- Because parents are children's first and best teachers, the role of libraries is to provide diverse collections, programs, and technical resources for young children, parents, and adults who work with families.

- Libraries build on family strengths and offer learning opportunities that reflect the interests, cultures, and needs of young children and their families.

- The library environment ensures a nonjudgmental, integrated, and interdisciplinary approach to lifelong learning that fosters the development of the whole person, whether child or adult.

- The diverse array of accessible collections, services, programs, and technical resources fosters a child's focused participation, creativity, critical thinking ability, cooperation, and problem-solving skills and supports the concept of self-motivated lifelong learning that ensures both children and adults the expectations of success.

### Libraries and the Building of Community

- Libraries help build family centered communities that nurture and support families with young children from the prenatal period throughout childhood and work collaboratively with local agencies to provide networks and referral services to enhance and promote family wellness and a healthy, stable neighborhood.

- The library's environment, policies, and practices support the natural human desire for learning and self-esteem. It encourages the recognition that the process of working with children and adults within the community is a learning process.

- The social and physical environment of the library models the acceptance and value of diverse cultures and perspectives, and of individual learning styles, abilities, and needs. It fosters a cooperative spirit among librarians, parents, community members, and professionals who serve young children and their families."

- Professional development of librarians is related to the needs and interests of individuals and to the library's vision and mission of service for families with young children and family service professionals. The library staff acts with respect, dignity, trust, and fairness toward all members of the community, is familiar with families within the community, and is aware of the ways in which young children and parents learn.

### Evaluation and Assessment

- Ongoing evaluation and assessment of services for young children and their families will lead to better practices in the learning environment of the public library and will increase the appropriateness and responsiveness of the library to the needs of individuals, families, and the community.

- The quality of service that a public library provides to children, families, and the community can be assessed by focusing on the essential elements including social environment, physical environment, parent participation, collaborations and networks, professional development, and administration.

### References

*Background paper in support of the Regents policy statement on early childhood.* 1993. Albany: New York State Board of Regents.

Bredekamp, S. 1987. *Developmentally appropriate practice in early childhood programs serving children from birth through age eight.* Washington, D.C.: National Association for the Education of Young Children.

*The Early Childhood Quality Review Initiative for public libraries.* 1995. Centereach, N.Y.: Middle Country Public Library.

Immroth, B. F., and V. Ash-Geisler, eds. 1995. *Achieving school readiness.* Chicago: American Library Association.

*Kids need libraries: Implementing the national goals for education through library services.* 1991. Chicago: American Library Association.

*Library Bill of Rights.* Rev. ed. 1982. Chicago: American Library Association.

*Realities: Educational reform in a learning society.* 1984. Chicago: American Library Association.

*Supporting young children and families: A Regents policy statement on early childhood.* 1992. Albany: New York State Board of Regents.

interpret their child's experiences and observing the child engrossed in the learning process can tell us a great deal about how a child may be perceiving the library experience. The *outside-inside perspective* refers to how the parent relates to the library and the *inside perspective* focuses on colleague relationships, staff-to-parent relationships, and staff/library relationships.

# ASSESSMENT OF PROFESSIONAL DEVELOPMENT

The Early Childhood Quality Review process outlined in chapters 8 through 11 focuses on these multiple perspectives. No matter which component is in focus or what strategies are selected, the library staff will learn about their library's strengths and areas of concern. The individual librarian, the library staff, and the library as a changing institution will all benefit as they apply the process and begin to assess the quality of service to young children and their families.

In pursuit of "better practice," the professional children's librarian needs to acknowledge personal responsibility for assessing one's skills and abilities. In addition to the Early Childhood Quality Review process, a *Self-Assessment Guide for Children's Services* (1994) and the *Self-Study for Children's Librarian* in Feinberg and Feldman (1995) are two useful self-evaluation tools that a librarian can follow as a guide for personal growth. Through continuous self-reflection and consideration of one's own strengths and weaknesses, librarians can bring to the library profession models of family centered practice. It is through such analysis that libraries and librarians will evolve a set of standards.

No matter the particular library, children's librarians need to accept responsibility for the social environment and interactions that occur within their library setting. Specific tools that apply to professional development include forms B-2, B-6, B-7, B-9, B-11, C-1, C-2, C-3, C-4, C-5, C-7, and D-10.

REFERENCES

Feinberg, S., and S. Feldman. 1995. *Serving families and children through partnerships: A how-to-do-it manual for librarians.* New York: Neal-Schuman.

Gestwicki, C. 1995. *Developmentally appropriate practice: Curriculum and development in early education.* Albany, N.Y.: Delmar.

Katz, L. G. 1997. "Multiple perspectives on the quality of early childhood programs." *ERIC Digest:* EDO-PS-93-2 (February 28): 1–5.

*Self-assessment guide for children's services.* 1994. Chicago: American Library Association.

# The Early Childhood Quality Review

# 8

# Foundation for Change

The Early Childhood Quality Review (ECQR) is a self-evaluation process for libraries. Inspired by the *School Quality Review Initiative* (1983), this process focuses on library services targeted to young children and their families. The review instruments, modified and expanded to meet the particular circumstance of libraries, were based on models in the fields of library science, early childhood education, and early intervention. These are listed on page 96. Both the process and instruments were field tested in five public libraries (*Early Childhood Quality Review Initiative for Public Libraries* 1995). Implementing the review process and using the various strategies, protocols, and tools will help librarians gain a more thorough understanding of appropriate spaces and services for young children and a knowledge base from which to identify "better practice" in the library setting.

## THE EVALUATION IMPERATIVE: VALIDATING THE LIBRARY'S ROLE

As librarians begin to focus resources on early childhood, they are faced with an evaluation imperative. In order to justify increased expenditure in this area and in order to validate the role of the librarian as educator, librarians need to examine the elements of library-based early childhood service. The ECQR provides practical strategies for gathering information to help identify, improve, modify, and re-create developmentally appropriate, family centered service within the library environment. Implementing a review will inform and

## DEVELOPMENT OF THE ECQR INSTRUMENTS
### Bibliography

Bredekamp, S. 1987. *Developmentally appropriate practice in early childhood programs serving children from birth through age eight.* Washington, D.C.: National Association for the Education of Young Children.

*Draft action plan to implement the Regents early childhood policy.* 1993. Albany: New York State Board of Regents (February).

*Early childhood education program evaluation 1992–1993.* 1994. Des Moines, Iowa: Independent Community School District: Department of Information Management.

Gaetz, J., et al. 1987. *To be the best that we can be: A self-study guide for early childhood special education programs and staff.* ERIC, ED320040.

Harms, T., and R. M. Clifford. 1980. *Early childhood environment rating scale.* New York: Teachers College Press.

Harms, T., D. Cryer, and R. M. Clifford. 1990. *Infant/ toddler environment rating scale.* New York: Teachers College Press.

*Head Start on-site program review instrument* (OSPRI). 1993. Palo Alto, Calif.: Community Development Institute.

*Programming for very young children.* 1980. Chicago: American Library Association, Association for Library Service to Children.

Robbins, J., et al. 1990. *Evaluation strategies and techniques for public library children's services: A sourcebook.* Madison: School of Library and Information Studies, University of Wisconsin.

Self-evaluation: Early childhood teacher. 1989. *Child Care Information Exchange* 66 (April): 19–20.

Willet, H. G. 1991. *Environment rating scale for public library children's services.* Chapel Hill: University of North Carolina (work in progress).

Young, D. 1984. Evaluating children's services. *Public Libraries* (spring): 20–22.

provide the foundation for change in a cooperative and productive manner, drawing on the strengths of individual librarians, staff, and administrators.

The ECQR framework is flexible, adaptable, and practical. It provides a complement to the long-range planning process already implemented by many public libraries. Successful use depends on the time spent conducting the review, the commitment to change on the part of the library, and the willingness of the staff, administration, and community to serve as critical friends and active participants.

## PURPOSE AND OUTCOMES

The ECQR engages the staff in a set of activities that are intended to generate a common vision of the library and its service to young children and families. It encourages self-reflection and helps to establish a culture of review. The process identifies the strengths and areas of concern relevant to a library's early childhood service and provides opportunities to share information and perceptions about library policies and practices. By creating an atmosphere of collaboration, the ECQR helps the staff reach a collective perspective and define future courses of action. Guided by the basic assumptions outlined in chapter 7 (see p. 91), the review is grounded in the examination of six essential elements germane to library-based early childhood service. A self-review report is prepared to document the collective perspective of the ECQR team and provide information to share with the library board, staff, and the greater community.

The self-review report describes a strategy for continuous improvement in the area of children's services and outlines a plan for staff development activities. It should become a part of the management data used for program development, budgets, evaluation, and the library's long-range plan. Each review is unique and each set of activities reflects an individual library's distinctive culture and environment.

## PROFESSIONAL DEVELOPMENT

An ECQR is particularly successful if leadership for its implementation emanates from the children's services staff. It is important that "better practice" be determined not by what librarians think should happen, but by how the library is actually being used and how children learn within the library environment. Staff involvement is a major force behind any change. It is critical to the self-review process, ensuring the integration of ongoing evaluation and assessment in the development of library service.

A willingness to change is part of the underlying philosophy required before the review can take place. Because it takes energy and time to conduct a thoughtful review and because there may be significant questions on the part of the librarians and staff as to the impact of the review on their work life, it is important for librarians and staff to have a clear understanding of how the information that is gathered will impact them. From the beginning of the review process, librarians and staff need to know how and to what extent the review process will affect individual performance evaluations and work assignments. Through involvement in the self-review, library staff can better understand the part they play in the learning process and ascertain their own areas of strength and weakness.

Conducting a self-assessment may be threatening to some staff members, particularly if they feel that they are being judged as individuals or that, through individual observation, their own performance will be evaluated. When first initiating the review within the library, it is important to understand that what is being evaluated is the *collective perspective* on how the library provides service to young children and their families, not the performance of particular individuals. Maintaining open lines of communication, building trust, and involving staff in the process help to dispel the idea that individuals are being judged. Involvement of the entire children's staff is essential.

# Involving Staff and Community

To enhance the review process, children's librarians are encouraged to garner support and local expertise from other departments and within the community. Integrating an array of participants such as adult and technical services staff, administrators, board members and Friends, parents, early childhood specialists, university professionals and students, a family development specialist, or a children's services consultant broadens the team's perspective and lends credibility and objectivity to the process.

# Confidentiality

Confidentiality issues are relevant to both staff and patrons. It is extremely important that patrons understand the voluntary nature of participation in the review process. The integrity and privacy of those participating in the review must be respected and protected.

Patrons have the right to know that their information will remain confidential, whether it takes the form of recorded behavior or expressions of opinions, ideas, and perceptions. They should be told how the information will be used and the extent of participation that is expected. Except where particular permission has been granted, reports or summaries of the review should not reveal individual identities.

# STAGES OF THE REVIEW PROCESS

When reviewing teaching and learning in the public library setting, primary concerns will be (1) the experiences of children and parents, (2) the opportunities provided for teaching and learning as they pertain to librarians, (3) the achievements of the children's services department, and (4) the benefits to the community.

The review process falls into three broad overlapping stages: preparation, implementation, and evaluation. Altogether these stages encompass:

- sharing information about the Early Childhood Quality Review;
- determining the review schedule;
- identifying a team;
- selecting priorities for study;
- assessing the present status through a portfolio review of current documents and materials;
- examining at least one element through selected data-gathering strategies;
- evaluating data throughout the review process;

- developing a collective perspective;
- organizing and implementing a course of action; and
- restarting.

## Sharing Information

The first part of the review involves the determination of avenues for sharing information about the review process both internally and externally. Having an appreciation of the overall goals and the role of each participant will not only enhance the process but will also provide the foundation for an ethical approach to information gathering. Determining when the review will take place, selecting members of the Quality Review Team, informing and involving the staff, board, and community are critical to the success of the ECQR.

Each library determines the time period for review and the extent of the review it will conduct. The review may be conducted over a multi-year cycle, focusing on different elements in each portion of the cycle. Or a library may conduct a thorough review encompassing several elements, resolving issues on a continuing basis. Each library needs to decide its initial approach and be prepared to modify some goals as the process takes shape.

## Identifying a Team

Once a library has decided to undertake a review, the first step is to form a Quality Review Team, which assumes the major responsibility for implementing the process. Under the direction of a team leader (most likely the department head), the review involves the entire children's services staff and selected others in its assessment of teaching and learning within the library. The roles, responsibilities, and composition of the team are discussed in chapter 9. All participants need to value and support diversity in libraries and the communities they serve.

Collecting data through strategies and methods outlined in chapters 10 and 11 enables the staff to identify their common understanding of the strengths of early childhood and family centered service within the library, as well as the areas in need of improvement. Through vigorous discourse and active participation, team members will begin to identify "better practice" within their own library.

## Selecting Priorities for Study

The review focuses on the examination of six essential elements: (1) physical environment, (2) social environment, (3) parent participation, (4) collaborations and networks, (5) administration, and (6) professional development. It is highly recommended that only one or two elements be selected for examination during any single review cycle. Understanding the nature of each individual element and its relationship to the library as a learning institution for young children is invaluable to the evolution of "better practice." However, none of these elements operates in a vacuum. A review of one element often reveals issues connected with another element. All review cycles explore and define the values, goals, and philosophies of the particular library as well as the way these are communicated to librarians, staff, patrons, and the community at large.

Gathering information about library service to children and families employs a range of strategies. These are based on the appropriateness for the evaluation of particular elements. Some suggested strategies include:

- conducting observations in specific public service areas of the library and during programs using checklists and observation protocols;
- analyzing existing written documentation, including policies and procedures, program and staff schedules, job descriptions, archived patron surveys and program evaluations, publicity materials and newsletters, statistical and annual reports, budgets, and long-range plans;
- conducting structured and open-ended interviews and focus groups with staff and patrons;
- distributing user feedback tools including surveys and questionnaires;
- reviewing children's work and library materials produced for young children and families;
- analyzing staffing patterns, including observed desk and room coverage;
- studying the number and types of reference questions, number and types of users, circulation and use of materials, and other output measures;
- observing the availability and integration of technology and the types of collections and exhibits or displays;
- documenting collaborations with other agencies and groups.

In addition, the review process may explore a key aspect of the collections or program offerings, or focus on accessibility issues such as a philosophy of inclusion, access for the disabled, or the variety and range of collection formats.

## Preparing for the Review

Individuals, families, and the entire library community will be affected by the review process. To prepare patrons and staff for the upcoming inquiry, it is essential to share information about the review weeks before the process begins. Making the staff, board, and patrons aware of sensitive issues and concerns during the fact-finding stages of the initiative is critical to its success.

# Working toward a Collective Perspective

Throughout the review process, the team will move toward achieving a collective perspective on the work they have seen and discussed. The collective perspective may take the shape of a working document, an action plan, or a comprehensive report. The information may be shared with library administrators, staff, library boards, and the greater community orally, in a written summary, or in a comprehensive report. The self-review report should present the collective perspective.

# DEVELOPING A CULTURE OF REVIEW

The ECQR promotes the development of a culture of review in public libraries. It is anticipated that such a culture will support and strengthen the children's services staff, as they extend their knowledge and understanding of the particular library in which they work and as they build capacity to meet the increasingly high standards, diverse needs, and growing expectations of families and young children in their community.

In seeking to develop a culture of review, the library's staff needs to enter into a self-determined review cycle, during which it is expected that they will develop an ongoing and systematic program of self-review. The review cycle should include at least two distinct review periods—most likely summer and fall or winter. Observing programs scheduled in a series format requires that observations take place over several weeks.

Reviews must be conducted in a professional and collaborative manner, mindful of the realities and complexities of teaching and learning in a public library setting. In order to minimize any disruption of service, the entire team needs to make every effort to maintain normal routines during the period of review. Each review should focus on the particular features of the library and its children's department while maintaining an awareness of the other departments and functions in the library.

The review process, which is cyclical and continual, instills a culture of ongoing self-assessment that encourages reflective practices and collaboration. This process of self-review supports the recognition and improvement of teaching and learning in libraries and the role of public libraries in the field of early childhood education. A selected list of resources for further information on evaluation is provided on page 102.

## EVALUATION
### Selected Resources

Bentzen, W. 1997. *Seeing young children: A guide to observing and recording behaviors.* Third Edition. New York: Delmar.

Cosby, P., P. Worden, and D. Kee. 1989. *Research methods in human development.* Mountain View, Calif.: Mayfield Publishing Company.

Gaetz, J., et al. 1987. *To be the best that we can be: A self-study guide for early childhood special education programs and staff.* ERIC, ED320040.

Harms, T., and R. M. Clifford. 1980. *Early childhood environment rating scale.* New York: Teachers College Press.

Harms, T., D. Cryer, and R. M. Clifford. 1990. *Infant/ toddler environment rating scale.* New York: Teachers College Press.

Irwin, D. M., and M. M. Bushnell. 1980. *Observational strategies for child study.* New York: Holt, Rinehart and Winston.

Katz, L. 1988. Engaging children's minds: The implications of research for early childhood education. In *A resource guide to public school early childhood programs,* ed. C. Warger. Reston, Va.: Association for Supervision and Curriculum Development.

Krumsieg, K., and M. Baehr. 1996. *Foundations of learning.* Corvallis, Ore.: Pacific Crest Software.

Martin, S. 1994. *Take a look: Observation and portfolio assessment in early childhood.* New York: Addison-Wesley.

McAfee, P., and D. Leong. 1997. *Assessing and guiding young children's development and learning.* Needham Heights, Mass.: Allyn and Bacon.

Robbins, J., et al. 1990. *Evaluation strategies and techniques for public library children's services: A sourcebook.* Madison: School of Library and Information Studies, University of Wisconsin.

Self-evaluation: Early childhood teacher. 1989. *Child Care Information Exchange* 66 (April): 19–20.

Willet, H. G. 1991. *Environment rating scale for public library children's services.* Chapel Hill: University of North Carolina (work in progress).

## REFERENCES

*The Early Childhood Quality Review Initiative for public libraries.* 1995. Centereach, N.Y.: Middle Country Public Library.

*School Quality Review Initiative.* 1983. Albany: State Education Department, University of the State of New York.

# 9

# Initiating the Review Process

The review process provides a perspective on the teaching and learning that are taking place in the library. Throughout the review, the focus should be on the relationship between the library's stated mission and goals and the educational strategies and learning opportunities that are provided to children and their families.

Creating enthusiasm about a self-review and making a commitment to the review process are the first steps. To set the tone for an organized and well-managed evaluation, the administration and staff need to select a Quality Review Team, which will lead the review and administer the mechanics of the process. Scheduling, staffing, reproducing forms, distributing announcements, and assembling existing documents are examples of some of the organizational and logistical issues that will arise. Time is needed to gather data and to evaluate them through vigorous and candid discussion. A successful review requires a commitment of both time and energy to provide for an open exchange of ideas. The collective perspective that develops provides the foundation for future planning.

## SELECTING THE QUALITY REVIEW TEAM

A team of reviewers is best suited to the task of gathering and analyzing the information. At the beginning of the review process, it is important to determine which librarians, staff, and community experts are available to make up the review team. Although opportunities to incorporate additional participants into the review process may arise later, it is important to identify the essential team members from the onset.

**103**

# Team Composition

Team members should be drawn primarily from the library conducting the review. Though all the children's services staff needs to be involved in the review process at some level, selected librarians and staff members will form the core of the review team, along with representatives from adult services, administration, and perhaps the library system as a whole. It is important that the team include an individual who will provide administrative assistance.

The inclusion of representatives from the community and from other library service areas outside the children's department is critical to the self-review process. The core group can be supplemented by former children's librarians, early childhood professionals, professors of library science or human development, parent educators or elementary school teachers, members of social service agencies, community members, library trustees, parents, and students in the early childhood and library fields. These individuals should be chosen on the basis of their interest and involvement in the library and its children's services and because of the unique perspective they bring to the review.

The Quality Review Team may also include some partnership reviewers. These individuals have a limited involvement in the review process. They may participate in focus groups and interviews or by responding to program evaluation questionnaires. For the most part, partnership reviewers are *not* children's librarians or early childhood educators. This multifaceted approach to team formation and review participation allows for a range of perspectives and creates a broad base of support for the development of a culture of review. (See the sample letter for community or partnership reviewers opposite.)

Before establishing a review team in a system with multiple branches, the extent of the review process must be determined. Conducting the review in the main or central library and two or three selected branches may provide the children's services administration with the assessment information they need to produce change. It is recommended that the staff in each location where the ECQR is being conducted, be actively involved in the review and that change be allowed to occur as recommended by the review team. This process is critical as it allows each staff member to identify "better practices," recognize weaknesses, and institute a culture of review for their location and for themselves.

The exact size of the Quality Review Team will vary depending upon such factors as the size and complexity of the library, the diversity of services provided by the children's department and the number of elements selected for review. (See page 106 for the composition of the teams taking part in the field study.) Typically, Quality Review Teams range in size from five to ten members. In larger libraries, the core leadership of the team may oversee the review while other staff and community participants make up each branch's review team or perhaps several teams for examining different individual elements.

## SAMPLE LETTER
## FOR
## REVIEW TEAM PARTICIPANTS


Ms. Mary Smith
Little Tots Day Care Center
St. Mark's Episcopal Church
208 Concord Avenue
Blue Ridge, NY 11843

Dear Mary,

Thank you for agreeing to be a member of our Early Childhood Quality Review Team. The Early Childhood Quality Review is designed to assist the library in assessing the quality and nature of teaching and learning it provides to its community through public library service. For purposes of this initiative, community is defined as children, birth through eight years; parents of young children; and the professionals who work with either or both of these groups. The aim of the review is to be helpful and supportive.

As a member, your commitment will be (1) to meet with the team on a weekly basis; (2) to conduct interviews (from a specific set of interview questions), observe (directly observe while taking notes without any interaction), and write up reports based on these observations and interviews; and (3) to work with the team to discuss and develop a collective perspective (a common viewpoint of the areas of strength and concern) of the library's early childhood service.

Our first meeting will take place in the Children's Department on Thursday, November 2 at 2:30 p.m. Please bring your calendar so we can plan our meeting schedule.

Again, thank you for agreeing to take part in this venture. We are all excited about this project and welcome your unique perspective.


Sincerely,

Carey Jones
Head of Children's Services

## SAMPLE TEAMS

During the field study, the five libraries organized their teams on the basis of the size of their children's staff and their ability to integrate participants from the community. All of the libraries involved their entire children's staff and at least one representative from the adult and/or administrative staffs. All of the libraries involved parents as partnership reviewers.

### Newburgh Public Library

Two children's librarians
Two adult librarians

### North Shore Public Library

Head of children's services
Two children's librarians
Three children's services pages
Library director
One reference/young adult librarian
One circulation clerk
Three representatives of the Friends of the Library

### Mastics-Moriches-Shirley Community Library

Four children's librarians
Library director's administrative assistant
One clerk

### Patchogue Medford Library

Four children's services librarians
Two parents, one of whom was a homeschooling parent
One college student
One retired kindergarten teacher

### Middle Country Public Library

*Administrative Team*
Three children's librarians
Two administrators
One university professor
One college intern

*Core component teams*
Small teams were organized around each of four elements selected for review. These teams included children's librarians, two adult reference librarians, two administrators, four early childhood teachers, and several programming clerks. The university professor provided students to conduct observations.

# Roles and Responsibilities

All reviewers are responsible for understanding the library's mission and vision so that they are able to evaluate the accomplishments of children's services in relationship to these stated goals. Every member of the review team needs to appreciate the range of teaching opportunities and settings available in the library and understand the data collection strategies that are selected for use during the review process. Each member of the Quality Review Team should have an opportunity to participate in both the direct observation component of data gathering and in the discussion of data evaluation.

It is important that *all* team members have the opportunity to:

observe teaching and learning within a full range of public services including the children's reference desk, programs and workshops, special children's areas, the circulation desk, computer areas, and adult service areas;

interview children's librarians and library support staff
including clerks, custodians, pages, volunteers, and other
professionals;

solicit anecdotal feedback from users;

complete written observation reports on visits, interviews, and
observations;

analyze children's work and the library portfolio;

participate in team meetings to share ideas;

participate in development of the collective perspective;

provide input into the self-review report.

Individual team members can accept specific responsibility for facets of
the review such as gathering children's work, assisting with schedules,
or working with focus groups.

## The team leader

The team leader is the person responsible for the overall conduct of the
review. While maintaining ongoing contact with the wider library community, the team leader has the responsibility for determining the
Review Team participants and their specific tasks, implementing the
review, and guiding the selection of data-collection strategies and the
development of the collective perspective. It is the job of the team
leader to communicate self-review study outcomes to the director,
administrators, and the community.

To be effective, the team leader needs to have an understanding of
the relationship between collections, programming and service content,
and assessment. In most cases, the team leader will be the head of the
children's services department or a librarian who has a basic knowledge and understanding of children's services in public libraries and
appreciates the learning process in the library context. The team leader
should be chosen for his or her ability to collaborate with a variety of
people, to observe and listen objectively and nonjudgmentally, and to
communicate orally and in writing. Cognitive flexibility, respect for
confidentiality, and organizational skills are assets in this role. Form
A-1 in Part Three lists the specific responsibilities of the team leader.

## Representatives from adult services and library system

It is recommended that each Quality Review Team should include at
least one person who can look at the library as a whole with a good
perspective of administrative issues and familiarity with adult collections and services. If the library undertaking the review is part of a large
library system, it is important to include at least one member who can
provide a system-wide perspective. Although these roles will usually be

filled by librarians or staff members, they could also be filled by representatives from a state or county library association or by a public library administrator. A large team may include more than one member with this expertise.

Adult services librarians, administrators, and system representatives should be full members of the Quality Review Team. They need to participate in all aspects of data gathering and analysis, the development of the collective perspective, and the creation of the self-review report. It is expected that these team members will attend all meetings, assist with the management of the review, and work with the team to ensure that all appropriate aspects of the library and library system are covered by the self-review study.

## *The administrative assistant*

Each Quality Review Team needs specifically assigned administrative assistance to expedite the logistics of the review. This individual, a library secretary, clerk, or administrative assistant, provides direct management support to the team leader. See form A-2 for the job responsibilities of the administrative assistant.

## GENERAL GUIDELINES

A two-way flow of information must be established in order to maximize the value of the review. A base of information needs to be provided to the library staff, the administration, and the wider community about the review process and its purposes. The same stakeholders need to be involved in furnishing information to the review team throughout the review process.

Scheduling the review can prove to be a daunting task, even for those with excellent organizational skills. Most of the field site libraries found that conducting the review while maintaining service required flexibility and team work. The frequency of programs and activities as well as the library's physical layout is a factor in selecting an appropriate observational methodology and determining the review timetable. Because service activity is seasonal, reviews should be alternated annually between the fall or winter and summer seasons.

The length of the review period will be determined by the nature and number of elements to be reviewed during a particular cycle. Each element may require its own timetable for completion, including program schedules (if appropriate), and a meeting schedule for the review team, or subsets of the team.

At some specified time during the review period team members will explore a representative cross section of children's work and the library portfolio. It is important for all of this work to be available on this occasion.

# Initial Administrative Meeting

The team leader, selected children's staff, and representatives from administration and adult services need to convene an initial meeting. During this meeting, the following steps need to be taken:

1. Determine what additional members of the Quality Review Team are needed. The composition of the review team and other organizational factors should be agreed upon prior to initiating the review process.

2. Establish the particular element(s) to be reviewed and make a preliminary selection of data-collection strategies based on their appropriateness for gathering information about these elements. Meeting time should be set aside to review and compare the range of appropriate data-collection strategies available. During the review process additional strategies may be added if more information is required about a particular issue.

3. Decide on the documentation that will be included in the library portfolio and the method of assembling it and, if appropriate, whether examples of children's work need to be collected and collated.

4. Outline effective communication techniques that will be employed throughout the review process, both for the review itself and for external communications.

5. Assign responsibilities for the above tasks.

6. Determine the overall timetable for the review and plan such logistics as observational assignments, timing and locations of meetings, external communications, and staffing patterns.

While the focus of the review is children's services, other aspects of the library's service that have an impact on the quality of teaching and learning need to be considered. Responsibility for dealing with these aspects should be allocated during this initial meeting, including who will gather information throughout the review period and who will lead the discussion on these specific aspects at the team meetings.

# Initial Documentation Gathering

Documentation needs to be collated by the team leader, children's staff, and administration. Documentation provides an initial perspective on the library, its patrons, staff, and mission. It furnishes a snapshot of the library within the context of community and an overview of existing programs, services, and collections aimed at children, birth through eight years, and their parents. This documentation is the substance of the library portfolio. It initiates the review process and provides an opportunity to identify exemplary practices. It is important that it contain up-to-date information and descriptions of current policies and procedures. Form D-1 provides a list of portfolio documents.

The team needs to decide whether they will be examining samples of children's work. Selected team members should be assigned to collate a representative cross section of children's work and devise a method for reviewing the samples. Chapter 11 covers the procedures for examining children's work.

# Briefing Meeting

Once the review team members are identified and the library portfolio is assembled, details of the arrangements need to be discussed with the entire review team at a briefing meeting. This is the time to establish the ground rules for effective communication and the development of the collective perspective. At this meeting, the team leader needs to finalize the detailed schedule for the review period and ensure that all members of the team are aware of their precise roles and responsibilities.

# Preparation of Forms

Following the initial briefing meeting, the team leader—with the help of the administrative assistant and other designated team members—should prepare all necessary materials for the review team(s) and ensure that forms are copied and distributed to the participants. The specific forms that will be necessary are determined by the elements to be reviewed and the strategies and methods selected by the review team. Sample observation, interview, and document analysis forms and checklists are available in Part Three.

# Ongoing Discussions and Meetings

Adequate time is needed during the review period for a range of formal and informal communications including but not limited to:

- providing brief feedback to librarians after observations;
- consulting on library policy and procedures with library staff;
- exchanging information with librarians, administrators, nonprofessional staff, children, parents, caregivers, professionals who work with families, board members, and community members;
- organizing and comparing observation notes;
- attending regularly scheduled and occasionally unscheduled team meetings to deal with uncertainties and discrepancies;
- building the collective perspective.

The perspectives of individual team members will be expanded by the diversity of data gathered and the range of information shared. Throughout the course of the review, it is essential that members of the team meet on a regular basis to discuss their individual observations, the information they have gathered, and their emerging understandings. Team meetings need to be arranged on a weekly or biweekly basis throughout the review period.

Regularly scheduled discussions should focus on three major themes: (1) evidence of better practice, (2) areas of reflection, and (3) areas with insufficient information. Using this format, team members can identify areas that require further investigation, talk about their own observations that support the type of learning taking place within the library, and share and comment upon documentation that they have gathered. This is also a framework for raising concerns about the quality of service being provided to young children without focusing on individual staff performance.

After several meetings, the team members will begin to form an understanding about the strengths and weaknesses of the library's early childhood services and spaces. They will identify new directions for exploration and indicate where additional information is needed. Appropriate strategies for expanding or refining data gathering need to be determined at this juncture in order to clarify evidence or negate conclusions.

The process of gathering and sharing information, discussing evidence and issues should go on throughout the review process. The use of guided questions and protocols will focus the team during group exchanges and begin to point them toward action steps for change.

The growing consensus that results from the discussion process is the group's *collective perspective*. Meeting discussion guidelines are provided in forms A-4 through A-6.

In most cases, it will be necessary to provide temporary desk coverage for those staff members involved in the review process. During the field testing, the smaller field site libraries found it was extremely difficult to schedule adequate time for meetings and discussion. However, the staff members found that they began to discuss the review during lunch and breaks or even during slower times at the reference desk. Though the circumstances were not ideal, the librarians stated that they were still able to produce results and reflect on services in a meaningful way.

Another field site library was in the process of completing a building renovation that included the children's room. Because they were finishing up the early childhood area, the review provided some pertinent information that could be immediately implemented. Though it is not recommended that libraries conduct the review during or closely following construction, going through the process before the construction is initiated can provide the children's staff with valuable insights and practical ideas regarding the library's environment for young children.

# Review of the Library Portfolio

The library portfolio is an essential component of the early childhood review process. The purpose of this portfolio is to provide a portrait of the library with particular focus on children's services.

Individual review team members need to interact with the materials and respond and expand upon their initial reactions. This can be done in one of the weekly meetings or individually throughout the review period. The documentation contained in the portfolio may provide further evidence of the strengths or weaknesses of the library's early childhood service.

Review of the portfolio should take place in conjunction with the other evidence. Consideration should be given to the nature of the available information, as well as any missing information, the strengths of the services provided, and the evidence for better practices and areas for concern. Questions to consider when reviewing portfolio materials are found in form D-2.

# THE COLLECTIVE PERSPECTIVE

The collective perspective should provide thoughtful commentary that, in conjunction with output measures, creates powerful support for early childhood services. The main purpose of the quality review is to develop a program of "better practice" for serving young children, parents, and adults who work with families. As team members discuss their developing perspective, they should consider the documented strengths and evidence of "better practices," as well as changes or actions that might be initiated in response to the areas of concern that have been revealed. Suggested questions are provided in form A-6.

A critical feature of the collective perspective is that it reflect the consensus of the entire review team. It is not merely a set of individual views of the team members nor is it the conclusion of one dominant individual. Rather, it is the expression of the collective understanding of the entire review team, achieved through systematic observation and data collection and a rigorous exploration of the various experiences and understandings developed in the course of the review process. Developing a collective perspective involves an honest, nonjudgmental, and forthright sharing of experiences and understandings, a vigorous commitment to the resolution of any differences, and an explicit agreement to refrain from minority reports.

# THE SELF-REVIEW REPORT

When the team has been able to reach a collective perspective that accurately represents the areas of strength and areas of concern for the library, the Quality Review Team should address the writing of the self-review report. The self-review report represents a written record of the deliberation. It describes the responses by the staff, children, parents, and community to questions guiding the self-review process (form A-7).

The self-review report should describe a strategy for continuous improvement in the area of children's services and outline the delivery of staff development activities. These suggestions and guidelines can be incorporated into the library's long-range plan and be included in the management data needed for program and budget development. An outline for the development of a self-review report is provided in form A-8.

Developing a self-review report has a number of positive consequences. In creating a culture of review and an atmosphere of reflection, the process of discussion and information sharing is the critical feature. However, documenting the deliberation and collective perspective assists both the staff and the community to communicate their expectations and to develop a plan of action to continue the improvement of library service to young children and families.

# 10

# Observational Methodology

Analyzing the nature and quality of teaching and learning experiences for young children and their families within the library setting enables librarians and administrators to better understand the priorities and learning styles of these patrons. Decision makers can gain the critical insights and information necessary to appreciate better practices and improve services and settings based on this input. Ultimately the teaching and learning experience for young children and their families within the library will be enhanced and enriched.

The primary focus of the Early Childhood Quality Review is the examination of library experiences using various strategies that allow a review team to observe current practice, recognize "better practice," and gain insight into patron perceptions. Particular strategies are selected both to match human and financial resources and focus on areas of interest or concern.

Methodologies have different strengths and weaknesses. At each step of the process, the selection of the most suitable strategy should be based on a recognition of institutional and individual goals and an accurate assessment of the time available for the review. The approaches to gathering information about current practice, perceptions, and priorities fall into three broad categories: observing, questioning, and examining existing documents and products. Observation, one of the cornerstone methodologies of quality review, is described in this chapter. The next chapter covers questioning and examining existing documentation.

## ETHICAL CONSIDERATIONS

Individuals, families, and the entire library community will be affected by the self-review process. It is essential to prepare patrons and staff for the upcoming inquiry before the process begins. In particular, it is critical to make patrons aware of their options within the fact-finding stages of the initiative.

Personal or family histories may make some individuals hesitant about expressing their opinions or having their actions or the behavior of their children recorded. There may be concerns about having their picture identified or the possibility that they could lose library privileges if they do not cooperate with observers or interviewers. It is extremely important that patrons understand the voluntary nature of participation in the review process. Children, as well as adults, deserve respect in this area. In the case of children, observation of behavior or collection of products may require the parent's and child's consent.

From the onset, it is important to keep in mind that objective observations of teaching and learning are, by definition, nonjudgmental. They strive for clear, concise, and concrete descriptions of ongoing events. They provide both individuals and the institution with an unclouded view of what is actually occurring within a library program or in a defined physical area. Observations assist in developing an understanding of how programs and places are used and perceived by patrons. They provide a foundation of knowledge that can highlight "better practice" and articulate areas in need of improvement.

Firsthand observation of the physical and social environment and parent participation are components of the review process. Although librarians may be natural observers in their daily role within the library, the regular demands of patrons make it difficult to capture the range of interactions and patterns of use that occur. It is important to set aside time for conducting systematic and objective observations, particularly when environments and programs are familiar.

## BASIC RULES AND GUIDELINES FOR OBSERVATIONS

Each team member should have the opportunity to participate in the direct observation component of data gathering. In order to conduct the most consistent and informative observations, it is important to consider the following points:

1. *All* reviewers need to observe interactions with parents, children, and professionals.
2. Direct observation must be as objective and neutral as possible.
3. Direct and systematic observations are rule based. These rules must be clearly specified at the outset and adhered to both during the observation and at the time the observation material is recorded. Establishing observational parameters prior to the onset of the observations supports objectivity.
4. It is essential to notify staff and patrons prior to observing either or both of these groups. This may be done through oral or written communication.

5. Each library staff member should be observed in his or her many roles. Special care should be made to capture the informal interactions of staff with children, parents, teachers, and other professionals as they occur throughout the day.

6. Observers should find an inconspicuous location from which to record interactions to avoid interrupting the naturally occurring behavior. Even when preliminary information about the review process has been made available to patrons, both adults and children may be uncomfortable when the presence of an observer becomes known.

7. A schedule of observational assignments allows each of the reviewers to observe the multiple facets of teaching and learning. The observation schedule should include:

   • informal interactions of staff with children, parents, teachers, other professionals, and staff wherever they occur;

   • story time and other programs for parents and children, birth through eight years;

   • class visits by children in early childhood programs and primary grades;

   • large-group programs for the community and after-school groups serving young children and their families;

   • children's reference desk;

   • children's room and special learning areas;

   • outreach sites, including schools, hospitals, and day-care centers.

## RECORDING OBSERVATIONS

Observations may be recorded using a wide range of formats including checklists, running records, rating scales, and answers to directed questions. These forms, available in Part Three, are based on developmentally appropriate practice, health and safety guidelines for early childhood programs, and documents adapted from the *School Quality Review Initiative* (1983). Key issues have been culled from a range of early childhood resources, with formats that have been adapted for use in the public library setting. The checklists, observation protocols, and questions on observing children working can be used by reviewers to assist in recording ongoing observations or as document summaries to assist in data analysis.

## Checklists

Checklists capture information about the presence or absence of particular people, interactions, behavior, objects, or environmental features. The usefulness of checklists depends on the clarity with which each of the listed items has been defined. These definitions may include particular aspects of the physical setting or specific behaviors that can be described in sufficient detail. All members of the review team should agree on their meaning. Checklists may be used during time-sampling, event-sampling, tracking, or snapshot observations or to summarize information initially gained from multiple observational and examination strategies.

# Running Records

An objective handwritten description of sequentially occurring behavior as it unfolds in time is a *running record*. This involves writing, or in some instances speaking into a tape recorder, a succinct account of what a person does or says within the setting. The duration depends on the rules for observation that have been selected for the particular strategy being employed. This type of open recording allows the observer to indicate all observed actions and interactions.

Closed recording directs the observer to search for the presence or absence of particular categories of behavior. Observation protocols suggest categories of behavior that may be used as "points of departure" to sensitize observers to the presence of particular types of behavior within the library setting. It is important to remember that they are not exhaustive and should not limit records of other areas, behaviors or types of teaching and learning. "A Picture of Learning in Libraries" (p. 85) and forms C-1 and C-2 provide examples of observation guides.

# Rating Scales

Rating scales require judgments about the degree or extent to which a behavior or collection of environmental features is present. The two ends of the scale need to be operationally defined so as to represent opposite ends of a continuum. Each step represents a different amount or degree of some behavior, activity, or aspect of the environment.

Graphic scales display these steps as evenly spaced points on a line. The familiar semantic differential scale developed by Charles Osgood (Irwin and Bushnell 1980) uses terms such as "always," "often," "occasionally," "seldom," and "never" to describe frequency of behavior. Numerical scales express similar gradations using numbers from 1 to 7, often accompanied by additional operational definitions.

Using rating scales is a highly subjective method of recording observations. They are often influenced by raters' tendency to avoid extremes and select the middle of the scale when in doubt. Frequently, individuals find it difficult to consider each scale independently. Thus, ratings are influenced by the order and grouping of individual scales. Nevertheless, rating scales may be used productively along with other records of observations to gauge the match between perception and reality. They may also be used successfully as a tool for gaining insight into library patrons' perceptions of library services and environments.

A significant rating scale for evaluation of library services to young children (identified while designing the ECQR) is the *Environment Rating Scale for Public Library Children's Services* by Holly G. Willet (1991). Inspired by the rating scales for child care by Harms and Clifford (1980), the "E-Scale assumes that children's services has the goal of enhancing child development and that providing an environment that supports children will allow public libraries to have the kind of impact desired" (Willet 1992, 166). This scale covers many aspects of the library's environment including physical facilities, staff behavior and attitudes, collections, policies, and procedures.

According to the document's author, the scales are still not ready for publication. "Like the planning and evaluation process itself, designing the *Environment Rating Scale for Public Library Children's Services* continues to be an iterative cycle of development, testing, analysis, and redevelopment" (Willet 1992, 173). Some of the specific items of Willet's rating scale were used in the design of the ECQR checklists. The *Environment Rating Scale for Public Library Children's Services,* when published, could provide a substantive complement to the checklists and protocols provided in this book.

## Answers to Directed Questions

A set of questions may be developed to cue an observer to look for and record particular kinds of behavior within a setting. The questions may vary in objectivity. Questions that require the observer to document personal insights gained during the observation may assist reviewers in their own education and professional development during the course of the review process. The traditional method for evaluating work with adults and school-age children focuses on the end product of the endeavor. Whereas early childhood professionals have long understood that participation in the learning experience is of great significance to the young child, it is only recently that educators working with teenagers and young adults have recognized the importance of articulating and evaluating the process of learning to learn (Krumsieg and Baehr 1996).

Collecting children's products as the sole measure of the learning experience inappropriately places an emphasis on uniformity. This focuses the goal on the program's ability to generate products that satisfy adult needs rather than to encourage children to experiment, discover connections, build concepts, and express their own individuality.

Answering directed questions provides an alternative or supplement to a library self-evaluation based on children's products. In observing children working, directed questions help focus attention on the child's behavior and involvement in the process. They encourage librarians to consider the full range of learning, problem-solving and developmental domains including: socio-emotional, cognitive, language, and motor areas, as well as the kinds of inferences that can be made about the nature of children's learning experiences based on direct observations.

Lilian Katz's (1988) categories for types of learning provide a useful frame of reference. She clearly distinguishes between attitudes toward learning, the acquisition of specific facts and concepts, the practice of particular skills, and the development of particular feelings associated with the learning experience.

A set of directed questions and recording guidelines are provided in form C-2.

# OBSERVATIONAL METHODS
## Time Sampling

Although all direct observations have natural time limits, such as the beginning and end of a program or class visit, time sampling incorporates time parameters throughout the entire observation as a means for enhancing objectivity. A watch or timer is used in order to divide the observational period into equally spaced units of time. These units can be as short as ten to thirty seconds or as long as twenty to thirty minutes.

The observer identifies a limited area such as a computer learning center or the children's reference desk as the focal point for the predetermined time period. She or he then takes a position that allows a clear view of the area but is somewhat removed from the center of activities.

Once the observation begins, the observer records actions and behaviors as objectively as possible without interfering. If more than one person is using an area, the observer needs to establish an observational order, determining which person will be the focus of the first observation, who will be the focus of the second observation, and so forth. This sequence can then be repeated throughout the observation. As people enter the setting, they can be added to the rotation.

Recording can be continuous or discontinuous. The record may be handwritten, videotaped, or spoken into a tape recorder. Alternatively, a checklist of concisely defined behaviors may be used. It is important that concrete examples of the specific behavior be connected to each item on the checklist. These operational definitions are used to maximize the likelihood of agreement among observers.

During the field testing, some librarians found that they preferred to record behaviors in a running record format and later refer to the appropriate checklist to help clarify their observations. Others preferred to use the checklist, recording comments on the side as part of their recorded observation.

# Event Sampling

Event sampling recognizes the regular occurrence of significant complex exchanges, each with its own inherent order and duration. For example, a request for assistance at the reference desk could be considered a regularly occurring event. It contains aspects of greeting, listening, and responding. Even this small event has a beginning, middle, and end. Events may occur within programs, such as a fingerplay demonstration as part of a story time or an introduction to finding books that is included in a class visit. Event sampling is also a way to hone in on such interactions as providing children information about the appropriate limits of behavior. Event sampling allows an observer to focus on discrete patterns within the large context.

There is a great deal of latitude in conceptualizing and defining events, which allows both individual and group activities to be captured in this manner. Prior to the onset, observers electing this form of observation need to have a clear understanding as to which particular objective behaviors mark the beginning and end of an event. These key landmarks should be discussed and understood by all those members of a review team studying similar events. During an event sampling observation, these well-defined entry and exit points are recorded in addition to the intervening exchanges and interactions.

As with time sampling, the choice of recording method is separate from the observational methodology. Running narratives, checklists, or directed question forms can be used to record an event. Handwritten notes can record antecedent and consequent actions. Recording the beginning and ending time of an event is a way of comparing the length or duration of the event in different contexts. Predetermining the time boundaries of event sampling allows an observer to come away from the observation with information about frequency of occurrence.

# Shadowing, Tracking, and Mapping

These combined observational and recording strategies enable the observer to understand the way in which children and adults sequence and pace their activities and actions within the environment. Staff members can be shadowed to get a better understanding of their routine experiences and recurrent job responsibilities.

Shadowing is a useful means of mapping patterns of staff-patron interaction. This requires that an individual patron or group (such as a family cluster) be met at the entrance to the library. The observer then follows the individual, dyad, or group as they move about the library. An objective record of their behavior may be written in narrative form in real time.

If a map of the library environment is created prior to the observation, the path of individuals can be marked on the map. Different colors may be used to indicate individuals, groups of different sizes, or children of different ages. Eventually, transparencies showing the alternate routes can be placed over the map, enabling the review team to gain a better understanding of the natural paths within the environment or the attractiveness of different areas to patrons.

A variant on these methods combines tracking or marking a path on a map of the environment with event sampling. In this case the event is defined by the cessation of movement and the onset of another activity such as interacting with an individual, a portion of the collection, or a particular feature of the physical environment. Stopping points should be clearly marked on the map and a description recorded of the behavior or action at each point.

# Anecdotal Observations

Frequently, interesting examples of teaching and learning are noticed during the course of other activities and responsibilities. When records of these observations are made after the fact, sometimes hours or days later, they are referred to as "anecdotal observations." Observations of the type are the most subjective of behavioral records. For this reason, they are recommended only for capturing preliminary or illustrative exchanges or events. They might be used to support the rationale for initiating the self-review process or requested to supplement the work of the review team and engage additional staff in the self-review process.

# Snapshot Observations

Controlling the sources of variation is a hallmark of systematic observations. This can be done by specifying the focus and time of the observation and the method and time of recording. Creating and following such rules can transform short observations of typical incidents into "snapshot observations." The reliability of this source of information is influenced by the immediacy of the record and the degree to which selections of location and range of activities or social groups are predetermined. A trained observer may enter or walk through an area at regular intervals and record observed behaviors, interactions, and comments. The physical record could be carried unobtrusively in a pocket or among other papers.

These time- and focus-controlled snapshot observations can be recorded in running narrative or checklist form. Since the nature of small public places can make it difficult for an observer (staff member) to remain outside the realm of activity, snapshot observations provide a less intrusive observational methodology that may prove particularly useful. With permission, a well-placed camera could be set to take pictures of an area at regular intervals. However, this would require both additional expense and additional time to analyze the photographs.

# REFERENCES

*The Early Childhood Quality Review Initiative for public libraries.* 1995. Centereach, N.Y.: Middle Country Public Library, 1995.

Harms, T., and R. M. Clifford. 1980. *Early childhood environment rating scale.* New York: Teachers College Press.

Irwin, D. M., and M. M. Bushnell. 1980. *Observational strategies for child study.* New York: Holt, Rinehart and Winston.

Katz, L. 1988. Engaging children's minds: The implications of research for early childhood education. In C. Warger, ed. *A resource guide to public school early childhood programs.* Reston, Va.: Association for Supervision and Curriculum Development.

Krumsieg, K., and M. Baehr. 1996. *Foundations of learning.* Corvallis, Ore.: Pacific Crest Software.

*School Quality Review Initiative.* 1983. Albany: State Education Department, University of the State of New York.

Willet, H. G. 1992. Designing an evaluation instrument. *Journal of Youth Services in Libraries* 5 (winter): 165–73.

Willet, H. G. 1991. *Environment rating scale for public library children's services.* Chapel Hill: University of North Carolina (work in progress).

# 11

# Interviewing and Examining Documentation

Observation is the cornerstone of the quality review. The techniques described in the previous chapter distinguish the Early Childhood Quality Review from other forms of evaluation and analysis. Using observational techniques in tandem with other assessment strategies adds greatly to the meaning and outcome of the review process. Quantitative statistical analysis can be carried out on systematically collected observational data. Standard comparisons and output measures, attitude assessment, and surveys are also very useful in creating a composite picture of the library's services and functionality. Additional sources for gathering quantitative data are available in the field of library science and can be applied when gathering support documentation relative to early childhood service.

This chapter describes interactive strategies that can be used to garner both quantitative and qualitative information. Through interviewing and examining documentation, the review process can provide further evidence in support of or reflecting on evidence of "better practice."

## THE PATRONS' PERCEPTIONS AND REFLECTIONS

Adults and some children may be able to provide additional information about their perceptions, attitudes, needs, and motivation through answers to written or oral questions. While planning this type of data gathering, it is important to keep in mind that both the physical and the social setting can influence the answers that people give to questions, as can the order of the questions. The backgrounds and attitudes of the people present, whether an individual is pressed for time or has the responsibility of caring for young children, all have a strong influence on responses. Even the way a question is phrased and presented can sway responses. People frequently attempt to select what they perceive to be the correct answer to a question or the answer that places them in the most positive light. "Yes" answers and answers that appear to agree with the perspective of the questioner are common.

The individuals or groups that are asked to participate in surveys, interviews, or focus groups will have a substantial impact on the impression that the review team receives. Reviewers need to be aware of group structures and demographic features when selecting participants and analyzing the information that they provide.

## Selecting Patrons

*Sampling,* or the process of choosing the individuals to represent the entire community served, is always an important issue. All interpretations grow from a knowledge of the nature of this defined group of people. The steps that are used in selecting the sample population should be rule governed. Knowledge of these rules provides knowledge of the sample. There are four main types of systematic sampling techniques: simple random sampling, stratified sampling, quota sampling, and purposive sampling.

Simple random sampling assumes that every individual has an equal likelihood of being selected. It does not make a distinction among different subgroups or ages within a population. This strategy for selecting survey recipients or members of a focus group would draw the population from a list of library users using a numerical pattern to determine the individuals selected.

When it is essential that particular subgroups within the population be included in the review, each identified category must be treated separately to ensure its inclusion in the sample. Categories such as age, gender, ethnicity, marital status, educational level, family role, area of residence, or number of years in the neighborhood may be useful categories for stratified sampling. Quota sampling uses the percentage of the group in the entire population as a basis for determining the proportion of each subgroup represented in the sample population. Alternatively, a purposive sampling strategy may be used which selects individuals based on specialized knowledge within a field or about the community (Berg 1995).

Nonrandom sampling is haphazard or fortuitous, based on convenience or propinquity. Although it may yield interesting insights into the activities and reactions of individuals, it is difficult to justify these responses as sufficiently representative of an entire population or community.

In the field site libraries, the population surveyed or interviewed was selected from regular users of programs and services. Parents of young children who regularly used library resources and services and professionals who either conducted programs or accessed collections made up the targeted samples.

# INSTRUMENTS FOR ASSESSING ATTITUDE
## Surveys

Standardized questions are the key to surveys. These questions are created in advance and in most instances the order of the questions is also predetermined. Requests for background information about the individual including gender, age, and community or group membership are generally included in the initial questions. The body of the survey may include questions that ask the individual to rate the frequency or quality of his or her own behavior, indicate the presence or absence of certain behaviors, describe beliefs, suggest ideas with or without a rationale, or prioritize future actions.

Surveys provide the opportunity to ask who, how, what, and why questions. Factual information obtained through "who" questions can help explain the ways in which segments of the community differ. "How" and "what" questions tap people's awareness and understanding of situations, likes and dislikes, and even thoughts about hypothetical or proposed changes (Bechtel, Marans, and Michelson 1987).

Surveys can be conducted orally or in writing through any and all means available, including but not limited to mail, flyers, e-mail distribution lists, hand delivery, distribution at programs, over the telephone, or in face-to-face individual exchanges. The number and content of the questions should be adjusted to the particular setting and participants. For example, surveys can be administered to staff and patrons in general or to some subset of the community that is served by the library. Survey-type instruments may also be useful as individual program evaluation tools or as part of a needs assessment.

## Interviews

The location, group size, and internal organization of the questions may vary during the questioning sessions known as interviews. *Field interviews* involve talking with individuals during the course of their everyday or naturally occurring activities. Examples include approaching a patron who has completed an inquiry at the reference desk or who has just returned borrowed books. These face-to-face interactions maintain the quality of a spontaneous social conversation. They may involve the interviewer providing information as well as seeking information. Such interviews will be strongly influenced by the setting, the nature of the activity that has been postponed or interrupted to handle the interview, and the skill and sensitivity of the interviewer. Alternatives to field interviews may involve appointments or scheduled meetings outside the flow of everyday activity. Any face-to-face interaction may be scripted to include closed or open-ended questions. In general, open-ended questions offer great latitude in approaching and answering the question.

Scripted interviews are basically oral presentations of surveys. The clinical interview format, on the other hand, allows the interviewer to adapt the questions to the needs, interests, and abilities of the person being interviewed. This leeway enables the interviewer to follow up answers to earlier questions or to change the wording and the order of the questions as necessary. The flexibility of a clinical interview is one of its strengths. Embedded within the strength, however, is the main weakness of this form of data gathering—its dependence on the ability of the interviewer both to construct questions and to build rapport during the course of the interview.

Interviews and written surveys may be administered to parents through distribution during programs, through personal contact in the children's room, or by phone. Similarly, interviews with individual staff members and/or professionals who run programs for the library can be conducted over the phone or in person, before or after a program, or during a separately scheduled meeting.

At the beginning of the review process, interview questions can provide a catalyst for self-reflection by the staff members. The interview process can assist individuals in thinking more about the library's services for young children and their individual role in implementing those services. The following questions can assist librarians involved in the ECQR process:

- What are the strengths of this library in serving young children and their families?
- How does the library support learning for young children and their families?
- What concerns or areas of reflection need to be considered when looking at the library's services and environment for young children?
- What recommendations do you have for changing the way the library serves children and families?

During the field testing, libraries employed both written and oral interviews with staff, parents, and professionals. Some of the questions were modified from the *School Quality Review Initiative* (1983). Other interview questions were constructed during the field testing. An array of interview question forms and checklists are provided in section B of Part Three. Some forms are applicable to all of the components under consideration. Others focus on specific elements such as parent participation or physical environment.

## Focus Group Interviews

Guided group discussions around a particular topic of concern or interest are a means of collecting information about behaviors, attitudes, and opinions (Berg 1995). These time-limited group interviews under the guidance of a facilitator can be extremely dynamic events, with participants building and expanding on one another's ideas and conversational topics. The process of group discussion may yield insights into the emotional content of topics and the perceived relationship between issues. Focus groups can be an effective means for "brainstorming" solutions to shared or interrelated problems.

Control of group membership is one strength of focus group interviews. The facilitator's function is to establish an environment that makes people feel comfortable speaking and sharing their opinions. The facilitator also acts as a moderator to prevent interpersonal conflict and dampen sources of intrapersonal stress surrounding controversial issues. It is best to chose a facilitator who is either an outside consultant or a staff member not directly involved in the provision of services to the targeted audience. This creates a more neutral approach to the interview process that encourages freedom of expression without risking the possibility that staff will want to respond to comments based on personal involvement with the issues.

Focus group interviews range from the presentation of a predetermined set of questions to an open-ended discussion of a general topic area. They may be preceded or followed by a set of survey questions related to the topic of interest. Asking focus group participants to answer written questions on the relevant topic prior to the discussion may provide important information to the facilitator about the position of individual group members. This background knowledge can then be used by the facilitator during the group process to draw out a minority opinion which might otherwise go undetected or become distorted in the face of dominant opposition.

Questionnaires or short surveys preceding focus group discussions may also assist each individual participant to gather his or her thoughts on a topic in preparation for the group exchange. Surveys administered following a focus group can reveal the impact of the discussion on the participants and make them aware of the value of their contributions to the self-review process.

Form B-12 in Part Three is a model of a focus group, including introductory remarks, questions, and guiding commentary.

# EXISTING DOCUMENTATION AND CONTENT ANALYSIS

The strategies employed in reviewing teaching and learning include a variety of methods for gathering information about library services to children and families beyond observing and questioning. Library and community documents are an important source of information. Examining children's materials and products is another strategy that provides invaluable information.

# Content Analysis

Objectively coding written and visual communication in order to reveal the patterns embedded in existing documents or products is the process of *content analysis*. This process requires the reviewer to create rules for recognizing patterns that are meaningful within the project's context. The first step is deciding which documents or products to analyze. All subsequent interpretations are determined by the degree to which the chosen documents or products accurately represent the entire range of materials.

Coding categories may be based on theoretical perspectives such as critical issues in human development and lifelong learning, or on principles of developmentally appropriate practices and family centered services. An alternative strategy for developing coding categories begins with immersion in the documents. This inductive approach is useful in identifying the issues, themes, and terms that are important to the individuals who created the documents, materials, or products. Both of these methods can successfully be used in tandem. An inductive approach to content analysis may be particularly helpful for analyzing the answers to open-ended questions from surveys, interviews, or focus groups and for looking at the products of children's workshops, such as stories, drawings, and artwork.

Depending on the nature of the documents or products and both the short- and long-range goals of the review, analysis may focus on either the *manifest* or the *latent* content of the material. The former content-analysis strategy emphasizes the outward structure or appearance of the document or product while the latter focuses on the conceptual and symbolic meaning of the work from the perspective of either the creator or the audience. Professional or discipline-based issues are frequently embedded within conceptual constructs. Like complex behavioral units, these jargon terms or phrases require operational definitions. For example, evidence of such constructs as "professionalism" and "acceptance of diversity" or "creativity" and "critical thinking" may best be approached through the analysis of latent content.

The selection of the units to be used in content analysis is intertwined with the process of defining coding categories. The units for analysis may be as small as individual words or as large as the entire item (document or product). The focus of the review will determine the level of meaningful analysis. When evaluating previously written material such as mission statements, long-range planning reports, job descriptions, circulars, or newsletters, it is important to keep in mind the audience to whom each message is addressed. Different interpretations may be reached depending on the perspective of the sender and the receiver. The amount of space devoted to relevant topics, the tone of the message, and the relative emphasis of different segments may yield important information.

Content analysis has several strengths that make it extremely useful for the library review process. Since it occurs behind the scenes and does not involve patrons, it can be easily scheduled. It poses less of a discomfort to individuals within the community than direct observation or interviews and does not carry the risk of interrupting the interactive process of service delivery. While its greatest strength comes from the ease with which it can be used on archival material, its weakness is its inadequate ability to portray individual differences in the implementation of current practices. Nevertheless, content analysis can enable reviewers to track the process of institutional change. The recognition of past patterns can be a starting point for the identification of "better practices" and the development of a culture of review and self-assessment.

During the field testing, one library assessed the element of administration. This particular element relies heavily on documentation. When examining documents, the review team focused on two key considerations: (1) How does this document(s) provide evidence of support for early childhood service? (2) What areas of reflection or concern can be identified after examining this document(s)?

# Types of Documentation

During the review process, it may be helpful to gather additional information about community demographics, areas of concern and need, and patterns of development and growth. The full range of library documents, policy statements, and long-range plans provides insight into the library's philosophy and the degree to which daily decisions support the stated mission. Examples of important documentation that may be relevant when examining the library's responsiveness to young children and families include:

> job descriptions and requirements
>
> diagrams of staffing and supervisory patterns
>
> personnel records identifying the areas of expertise and education of librarians and staff
>
> listings of opportunities for professional development
>
> written policies concerning patron registration, borrowing privileges, fines, responsibilities, and accessibility
>
> policies and procedures governing the selection of materials and the development of collections and programs
>
> descriptions of publicity and outreach plans and protocols
>
> mission statements
>
> all forms of annual and long-range planning reports and planning tools
>
> statistical analyses and reports of budget allocations
>
> records of reference questions, numbers and of types of users across a daily, weekly, and seasonal time frame
>
> records of computer use

copies of all circulars, announcements, and newsletters

past patron surveys and program evaluations (which may reveal unexpected patterns of communication, public and staff preferences, and ease of accessibility)

information about the library's coordination of services and collaborative activities with other community agencies and groups

children's products

The checklists in Part Three, section D outline other forms of documentation that may be relevant to particular elements.

Once these materials are collected, they may become part of the library portfolio. These materials will be instrumental in the creation of a profile of the library from the perspective of services for young children and their families. Chapter 9 discusses the importance of the library portfolio and each team member's responsibility in reviewing the materials it contains.

Questions for use in document analysis are provided in form D-3. This form and the portfolio questions form (D-2) can and should be used as the team works its way toward an understanding of particular elements as well as the development of a collective perspective. Documents often provide additional evidence that either supports or negates a review team's findings.

# REVIEWING CHILDREN'S WORK
## Procedures for Assembling Children's Work
### Nature of work

A sample of work from across the program and service spectrum should be collected. This need not be written work, but might include artwork, graphs or charts, or even audio- or videotapes. These types of products can be analyzed using content analysis methodology. Other samples of "work" can include reference questions and follow-ups that occurred, periodical requests, materials checked out in conjunction with a program or information request, computer searches, etc. An analysis may be available of the types and subjects of materials that have been requested or checked out.

### Assembling the work

It is suggested that one or more members of the staff be given the responsibility of assembling the collection of children's work. The collection should be representative of the program and services in the library, but the number of pieces will depend on the size of the library.

Materials may include current and/or recently produced items from a representative sample of regular and occasional program and library child patrons, birth through eight years. Joint productions of children and other family members or professionals who work with families should also be included. Within each age level, the samples should be representative of the library's programs and community. The work of a range of economic, educational, and ethnic backgrounds should be included. The samples should be packaged and labeled by general age level.

It is important that libraries receive permission from both parents and children to have their work reviewed. This request can be made orally or in writing.

## Procedures for Reviewing Children's Work

All reviewers should review children's work at some point during the process. Directed questions for observing children working can also be used to guide the content analysis of children's products and requests. (See form C-2.)

## Nature of findings

Reviewers should be prepared to share their tentative hypotheses about the nature of learning and program quality based on their analysis of these products and records. Such preliminary statements assist the review team in determining areas for further investigation. Hypotheses about the degree to which programs provide opportunities for creativity, critical thinking, skill development, language enhancement, and problem solving, as well as the variety of learning opportunities, the exposure to print and media, and the integration of technology are useful starting points for reflecting on the presence of cognitively enriching and developmentally appropriate experiences and materials. Reviewers may wish to revisit the collection of children's work several times during the review period to look for patterns that yield additional evidence confirming or negating developing perspectives.

REFERENCES

Bechtel, R., R. Marans, and W. Michelson, eds. 1987. *Methods in environmental and behavioral research.* New York: Van Nostrand Reinhold.

Berg, B. 1995. *Qualitative research methods for the social sciences.* 2nd ed. Needham Heights, Mass.: Allyn and Bacon.

*School Quality Review Initiative.* 1983. Albany: State Education Department, University of the State of New York.

# Quality
# Review
# Tools

# Review Process Guidelines

# A-1  Team Leader  ROLES AND RESPONSIBILITIES

The team leader is the person responsible for the overall conduct of the review. In many cases, the team leader will be the children's librarian or head of the children's services department.

Determining participants of the Early Childhood Quality Review Team (ECQR Team)

Meeting with the library staff and the wider community to discuss the review process

Arranging for the initial meetings of ECQR Team

Developing an overall schedule for the review

Interviewing administrators and supervisory personnel

Organizing and analyzing the library portfolio and children's work with team members

Maintaining communication with the library administration during the review

Conducting regular discussions with the review team members to assure that the review is proceeding without difficulty

Communicating the collective perspective to the director, staff, and community

Working with key members of the review team to complete the written review report

Other:

# A-2   Administrative Assistant   ROLES AND RESPONSIBILITIES

The administrative assistant is responsible for the logistics of the review.

Confirming the participation of all review team members in the scheduled review

Working with the team leader to set up meetings and to discuss the details of the review

Maintaining a journal of the review as it unfolds

Attending to all the details of the review in the library:

copying materials and forms

collating portfolio materials

preparing schedules

preparing and distributing forms and reports

arranging space for review team interviews/focus group meetings

Other:

# A-3   Initial Meeting

On this occasion particular attention should be given to the items listed below.

The element(s) to be examined

The initial strategies to be used to gather data

The time line for the review

The schedule for gathering data

Methods for notifying the general community about the schedules and strategies

Guidelines for effective communication and discussion during the review process

Need for additional ECQR team members or affiliate members

# A-4   Observation and Documentation Guidelines

The team leader draws up a schedule of observations and the framework for document analysis to reflect a reasonable coverage of all aspects of children's services.

The review team determines the most appropriate strategies for collecting information and reporting on any areas of special focus.

Selection of appropriate observational methodology should take into account the frequency of programs and activities as well as the library's physical layout.

When the review team conducts the review once each calendar year, reviews should be alternated annually between the fall or winter and summer months.

The length of the review process is based on the element(s) chosen as well as the number of elements to be reviewed during each cycle.

The composition of the review team and other organizational factors are agreed upon prior to the review.

At a specified time during the review period, a cross section of children's work and the library portfolio should be available for team members to examine.

# A-5  Weekly/Biweekly Meetings

Date _____  Reporter _____

Element(s) _____

A summary of each meeting of the review team should be recorded in writing, providing ongoing documentation of the review process as it unfolds.

Evidence of better practice:

Areas of reflection:

Areas for more information:

Suggestions for data-gathering strategies:

Meeting number _____  Date of next meeting _____

# A-6  Reaching a Collective Perspective

Date _____  Reporter _____

Element(s) _____

These questions serve as a guide to the review team as they begin to formulate a collective perspective. Questions can be discussed in group meetings as well as individually answered by team members.

Through your observations, what examples of better practice did you identify?

Through your observations, what areas of reflection or concern did you identify?

What recommendations for implementation of better practices within the library can you make?

Through your observations, what are the strengths that you can build upon?

What changes or actions can be initiated in response to this review process?

# A-7 Formulating a Self-Review Report

Date _____ Reporter _____

Element(s) _____

These questions serve as a guide to the review team as they begin to formulate the review report. They can be discussed in group meetings as well as individually answered by team members.

How does the library encourage and support the initiation of lifelong learning as presented in the values and assumptions?

What learning opportunities for young children, their families, and the professionals who work with them are available in our library?

Which of these opportunities are sources of pride?

Which areas are sources of concern?

What action plans are needed to continue our improvement?

What are the main insights about our library that we want to share with specific audiences?

# A-8  The Self-Review Report

In developing the self-review report, attention should be given to the items listed below.

1. **Description of Review Process**
   element(s)
   data-gathering strategies
   time line
   ECQR team
   other participants

2. **Sources of Information**
   a description of the library and its service to young children and their families
   the mission statement, goals, and priorities of the library and of the children's department
   a statement of philosophy/plan of service
   a community profile
   statistical information on library use by children and families

3. **Areas of Strength**
   physical environment
   social environment
   teaching and learning practices
   availability and use of resources
   staff development activities
   collaborations and partnerships with community agencies, formal and informal
   evaluations, feedback mechanisms
   other pertinent information

4. **Areas of Concern**
   physical environment
   social environment
   teaching and learning practices
   availability and use of resources
   staff development activities
   collaborations and partnerships with community agencies, formal and informal
   evaluations, feedback mechanisms
   other pertinent information

5. **Plan of Action**
   goals and objectives
   action steps
   time line
   next steps

# B

# Interview/Survey Tools

# B-1   Parent Interview

Date _____     Interviewer _____     Time: from _____ to _____

Type of Interview/Survey (check one)    ☐ in person    ☐ phone    ☐ self-administered

Element(s) _____

What programs, materials, and services do you and your young children use at the library?

How often do you use the library? attend programs? borrow materials?

How do you think the library helps you and your child learn? Can you give us any examples?

Please suggest additional ways the library can help you and your child.

_____

*This form may be adapted to use as a written survey and distributed in the children's room or during a program.*

# B-2   Professional/Staff Interview

Date _____     Interviewer _____     Time: from _____ to _____

Type of Interview/ Survey (check one)   ☐ in person   ☐ phone   ☐ self-administered

Element(s) _____

Using these questions to guide you, comment on the evidence of better practice and areas of reflection and concern regarding the library's service to young children and families based on your experience.

What are the strengths of the library in serving young children and their families?

How do parents support their young child's learning in this library?

How do parents participate and provide input or feedback in this library?

In what ways do parents serve as resource people for each other?

From your perspective do parents understand the goals and objectives of the library's programs/services/collections?

How do you feel this library supports the parent in the role of teacher?

How are parent suggestions handled in the context of programs or in the children's area?

What recommendations do you have for changing the way this library serves children and families?

Are there any other comments or suggestions you would like to make in relation to the content of this interview/survey?

# B-3   Administration/Professional Development

Date _____   Interviewer _____   Time: from _____ to _____

Type of Interview/ Survey (check one)   ☐ group   ☐ individual

Element(s) _____

Using these questions to guide you, comment on the evidence of better practice and areas of reflection or concern regarding the library's service to young children and families as demonstrated through documentation. Documentation can be gathered using the documentation checklists found in section D.

Does the library use data from the demographic profiles and community resources for planning or when determining long-range needs?

Does the children's services staff determine specific programs and services based on the demographic profile of the community?

Does the children's services staff determine specific programs and services based on the availability of other community resources for families and children?

Do library policies and procedures reflect a commitment to young children?

Are marketing efforts geared toward service for young children and families?

To what extent do user surveys, focus groups, newsletters, etc. reflect the library's children's services?

What is the percentage of time that the staff is involved with public services, planning, professional commitments, board work, community networks, etc.?

Estimate the ratio of children's staff to the entire library staff. What is the amount of staff time devoted to early childhood services?

Estimate the percentage of budget that is committed to children's services. What is the amount dedicated to early childhood and parenting services?

What professional literature is distributed and read among children's staff? How much is focused on early childhood and/or parenting?

Does the staff have adequate planning time to accomplish the department's goals?

What is the composition of staff qualifications? Are there any staff members who have had special training in early childhood or parent education?

What in-service training is available? Orientation for new staff? Continuing education on working with young children and families?

Are ongoing staff meetings provided?

# B-4   Social Environment

Date _____   Interviewer _____   Time: from _____ to _____

Program_____

Based on staff interviews, check **R**arely, **S**ometimes, or **F**requently. Refer to chapter 2 for description of appropriate behavior.

|  |  | R | S | F |
|---|---|---|---|---|
| 1. | Arranges the group in an appropriate fashion for the particular program | — | — | — |
| 2. | Schedules the same staff member to conduct the program within a series | — | — | — |
| 3. | Schedules length of program based on age of children | — | — | — |
| 4. | Maintains a routine and consistent format for each session | — | — | — |
| 5. | Has consistent, simple rules which are explained to children and parents | — | — | — |
| 6. | Allows children to participate in simple clean-up activities if necessary | — | — | — |
| 7. | Provides for individual, small group, and large group activities based on the age and attention span of the children | — | — | — |
| 8. | Emphasizes either peer group interactions or parent-child interactions, based on needs and age of children | — | — | — |
| 9. | Includes staff-directed and child-initiated activities | — | — | — |
| 10. | Reflects active and quiet time during program session | — | — | — |
| 11. | Reflects a well-planned schedule with a smooth transition from one activity to another | — | — | — |
| 12. | Offers a wide variety of language experiences including some of the following: picture books, songs and nursery rhymes, fingerplays, flannelboards, puppets, videos, dramatizations | — | — | — |
| 13. | Provides for repetition of familiar songs, fingerplays, stories, etc. within each program series | — | — | — |
| 14. | Emphasizes a visual focus | — | — | — |
| 15. | Emphasizes experiential learning relevant to life experiences and emotional needs | — | — | — |
| 16. | Includes lively and action-oriented activities | — | — | — |
| 17. | Integrates activities to foster motor development | — | — | — |
| 18. | Integrates art and music activities appropriate to the age of the children | — | — | — |
| 19. | Includes activities that encourage children to gain new skills | — | — | — |
| 20. | Provides a handout that includes a listing of stories and activities to encourage follow-up at home | — | — | — |
| 21. | Understands the importance of play as an appropriate learning medium for children and a critical component of programming | — | — | — |
| 22. | Plans programs that focus on emergent literacy skills and reading readiness | — | — | — |
| 23. | Prepares program materials prior to onset of programs including use of manipulative, audio and visual aids, and related circulating collections | — | — | — |
| 24. | Plans programs with a theme in mind | — | — | — |
| 25. | Designs programs to promote positive self-image and attitude toward peers | — | — | — |

# B-5  Physical Environment/Administration  HEALTH AND SAFETY

Date _____  Interviewer _____

Location _____

Based on staff interviews, check **Y**es, **N**o, or **N**ot **A**pplicable. In some instances, documents may be needed. Refer to chapter 3 for descriptive information.

|     |                                                                                                        | Y | N | NA |
|-----|--------------------------------------------------------------------------------------------------------|---|---|----|
| 1.  | Emergency phone numbers are clearly posted for staff                                                    | — | — | — |
| 2.  | Emergency procedures including clearly marked emergency exits are posted for staff                      | — | — | — |
| 3.  | Emergency lighting is available in case of power failure                                                | — | — | — |
| 4.  | Rooms are well lighted                                                                                  | — | — | — |
| 5.  | Electrical sockets are covered                                                                          | — | — | — |
| 6.  | Clearly defined pathways are free from obstruction                                                      | — | — | — |
| 7.  | Pathways are wheelchair accessible                                                                      | — | — | — |
| 8.  | Heating units are covered or out of reach                                                               | — | — | — |
| 9.  | Furniture has rounded corners                                                                           | — | — | — |
| 10. | Surfaces are smooth (free of splinters, protruding nails, broken or loose parts, and sharp edges)       | — | — | — |
| 11. | Equipment and materials in contact with children are clean                                              | — | — | — |
| 12. | Equipment and materials in contact with children are in working condition (repaired)                    | — | — | — |
| 13. | Upholstery is made of nonflammable material                                                             | — | — | — |
| 14. | Shelves are stable (and can support the additional weight of 50 lbs., if necessary)                     | — | — | — |
| 15. | Trash is contained within receptacle                                                                    | — | — | — |
| 16. | Trash receptacle openings cannot be reached by a toddler                                                | — | — | — |
| 17. | Drinking fountain is accessible to children's room                                                      | — | — | — |
| 18. | Drinking fountain is low enough for a young child to reach without assistance or a stepstool is available | — | — | — |
| 19. | Bathrooms are accessible to the children's room                                                         | — | — | — |
| 20. | Bathrooms are clean and disinfected daily or more frequently as necessary                               | — | — | — |
| 21. | Diaper changing facility is available in the women's room                                               | — | — | — |
| 22. | Diaper changing facility is available in the men's room                                                 | — | — | — |
| 23. | Stepstool is available for use in bathroom, if needed                                                   | — | — | — |
| 24. | Towel dispenser or dryer in bathroom is accessible to young children                                    | — | — | — |

## B-6 Parent Participation/Collaborations/ Professional Development/Social Environment

Date _____    Interviewer _____    Time: from _____ to _____

Source of Information (check one)    ☐ survey    ☐ interview    ☐ focus group

Based on interviews, surveys, and focus groups, check **R**arely, **S**ometimes, or **F**requently regarding staff attitudes and behaviors. Refer to chapter 5 for background descriptions.

|  |  | R | S | F |
|---|---|---|---|---|
| 1. | Respects parents as primary teachers of their child | — | — | — |
| 2. | Recognizes that the family is the constant in the child's life while the library staff fluctuates | — | — | — |
| 3. | Treats parents as partners in the development of library service | — | — | — |
| 4. | Facilitates the parent/professional partnership | — | — | — |
| 5. | Expresses support and empathy toward parents | — | — | — |
| 6. | Regularly uses active listening skills when working with parents | — | — | — |
| 7. | Communicates policies and practices to parents | — | — | — |
| 8. | Distributes information to new families in the community | — | — | — |
| 9. | Provides new families with an orientation to the library's services through a routine process | — | — | — |
| 10. | Encourages parents to act on their own behalf | — | — | — |
| 11. | Encourages parents to act on behalf of their children | — | — | — |
| 12. | Designs programs and collections to enhance parenting skills and confidence | — | — | — |
| 13. | Designs programs with parents and children in mind | — | — | — |
| 14. | Encourages parents to observe and/or participate with their children | — | — | — |
| 15. | Includes circulating materials in programs to extend early childhood learning to the home | — | — | — |
| 16. | Integrates materials for parents into children's programs | — | — | — |
| 17. | Integrates materials for children into parents' programs | — | — | — |
| 18. | Provides access to children's materials to help parents discuss difficult issues | — | — | — |
| 19. | Provides settings for parents to gather and interact informally | — | — | — |
| 20. | Provides formal setting for parents to share information and learn from each other and from professionals | — | — | — |
| 21. | Encourages parent-to-parent communication | — | — | — |
| 22. | Recognizes family strengths and diversity | — | — | — |
| 23. | Presents a variety of alternatives to encourage parent involvement in children's activities | — | — | — |
| 24. | Offers programs in parents' home language or provides translators as needed to facilitate parent participation | — | — | — |
| 25. | Offers alternative forms of communication and participation for parents with disabilities | — | — | — |

# B-7   Collaborations/Administration/Professional Development

Date _____   Interviewer _____

Information Source (check one)   ☐ staff   ☐ administrator   ☐ community representative

Type of Interview/Survey (check one)   ☐ in person   ☐ phone   ☐ self-administered

Based on interviews with staff and community representatives, check **R**arely, **S**ometimes, or **F**requently regarding the following library practices. Refer to chapter 5 for descriptive information.

|  |  | R | S | F |
|---|---|---|---|---|
| 1. | Reflects a commitment to outreach and coalition building | ___ | ___ | ___ |
| 2. | Works with other service agencies and organizations as part of an established process | ___ | ___ | ___ |
| 3. | Designates staff to coordinate services and programs between agencies | ___ | ___ | ___ |
| 4. | Participates in or initiates partnerships, collaborations, or appropriate community networks | ___ | ___ | ___ |
| 5. | Supports the community's information and referral system by developing, maintaining, or contributing to directories, databases, Web sites | ___ | ___ | ___ |
| 6. | Seeks joint funding opportunities to build and develop collaborative services | ___ | ___ | ___ |
| 7. | Addresses barriers to children or adults with special needs and encourages their participation in library services | ___ | ___ | ___ |
| 8. | Accesses information and referral directories, databases, or Web sites to serve families and readily refers parents to services | ___ | ___ | ___ |
| 9. | Integrates family literacy and family information literacy in children's services | ___ | ___ | ___ |
| 10. | Maintains a parent/professional information collection | ___ | ___ | ___ |
| 11. | Avoids duplication by designing programs and collections that serve as a complement to existing services or are not available in other local agencies | ___ | ___ | ___ |
| 12. | Provides outreach services to home day-care providers, child-care centers, shelters, hospitals, or other institutions that serve families and young children | ___ | ___ | ___ |
| 13. | Involves community agencies that work with families and young children in ongoing library-based programs | ___ | ___ | ___ |
| 14. | Markets library services, collections, and programs to professionals working with families and young children | ___ | ___ | ___ |
| 15. | Regularly disseminates information on library services and programs for children and families to outside agencies and organizations | ___ | ___ | ___ |
| 16. | Regularly disseminates information on community services and programs for children and families through the library | ___ | ___ | ___ |
| 17. | Uses children's programs as an opportunity to market other library services to parents | ___ | ___ | ___ |
| 18. | Participates in joint training opportunities to enhance professional skills | ___ | ___ | ___ |
| 19. | Provides training to outside agency staff | ___ | ___ | ___ |
| 20. | Participates in professional organizations | ___ | ___ | ___ |

# B-8  Administration

Date _____ Interviewer _____

Type of Interview/Survey (check one)    ☐ in person    ☐ phone    ☐ self-administered

Based on staff interviews, check **R**arely, **S**ometimes, or **F**requently regarding the following practices. Refer to chapter 6 for descriptive information.

|  |  | R | S | F |
|---|---|---|---|---|
| 1. | Uses data and information to determine long-term goals and short-term objectives for children's services | — | — | — |
| 2. | Examines the library's strategic plan and reviews elements that impact children's services | — | — | — |
| 3. | Outlines priorities and needs for early childhood in the library's long-range plan | — | — | — |
| 4. | Sets priorities for services, programs, and collection-development strategies to formulate an action plan | — | — | — |
| 5. | Addresses the needs of families and children with disabilities | — | — | — |
| 6. | Conducts periodic focus groups, user surveys, telephone surveys, and program evaluations to gather information relevant to service for young children and families | — | — | — |
| 7. | Enlists the support of the library administration or board for review and provision of services for young children and their families | — | — | — |
| 8. | Enlists the support and cooperation of other library departments to develop and promote collection and information services for young children, parents, and other adults who work with children | — | — | — |
| 9. | Enlists the support and cooperation of other library departments to develop and promote programs for young children, parents, and other adults who work with children | — | — | — |
| 10. | Claims sufficient amount of meeting-room space for children's department in relation to size of community and demand for early childhood programs | — | — | — |
| 11. | Uses a variety of media in programs and promotes the circulation of similar materials | — | — | — |
| 12. | Markets the importance of early childhood services | — | — | — |
| 13. | Nurtures positive media relations | — | — | — |
| 14. | Explores alternative funding opportunities, including grants and corporate sponsorships for collections, programs, and services for young children and their families | — | — | — |

# B-9   Administration/Professional Development
## PROGRAM DEVELOPMENT

Date _____      Interviewer _____

Type of Interview/Survey (check one)     ☐ in person     ☐ phone     ☐ self-administered

Based on staff interviews, check **R**arely, **S**ometimes, or **F**requently regarding the following practices. Refer to chapters 6 and 7 for descriptive information.

### Scope

|     |     | R | S | F |
|-----|-----|---|---|---|
| 1. | Offers programs developmentally sequenced from birth through age eight | — | — | — |
| 2. | Offers programs and services for infants and toddlers | — | — | — |
| 3. | Offers programs and services for preschool children | — | — | — |
| 4. | Offers a variety of formats such as parent-child, child only, parents only | — | — | — |
| 5. | Provides family programs on a regular basis | — | — | — |
| 6. | Coordinates programs with preschool education and child-care center providers | — | — | — |
| 7. | Coordinates programs with family home child-care providers | — | — | — |
| 8. | Provides alternative programs or activities for older siblings while younger children attend programs | — | — | — |

### Organization

| | | | | |
|-----|-----|---|---|---|
| 9. | Organizes programs to avoid scheduling conflicts | — | — | — |
| 10. | Produces an integrated staff schedule including reference desk and program coverage | — | — | — |
| 11. | Schedules programs on Saturdays and evenings for working parents and their children | — | — | — |
| 12. | Schedules programs for primary grade children after school and on weekends | — | — | — |
| 13. | Registers prior to programs | — | — | — |
| 14. | Limits number of children in programs based on age, space, and program content | — | — | — |
| 15. | Maintains attendance sheets for programs | — | — | — |
| 16. | Accommodates children on a waiting list when possible | — | — | — |

### Planning and Publicity

| | | | | |
|-----|-----|---|---|---|
| 17. | Prepares press releases and flyers on services and programs | — | — | — |
| 18. | Prepares handouts for programs on a regular basis | — | — | — |
| 19. | Informs parents about philosophy, content, and purpose of programs including any rules and/or guidelines prior to program either through a meeting or special mailing | — | — | — |
| 20. | Prepares curriculums, program resource listings, and guidelines for programs | — | — | — |
| 21. | Uses reference and professional materials to help plan programs | — | — | — |
| 22. | Designs written procedures for program planning and implementation | — | — | — |
| 23. | Understands the importance of serving the family unit in a holistic manner when designing and planning programs for young children | R | S | — |
| 24. | Designs services to provide emotional support to meet the needs of families | — | — | — |
| 25. | Analyzes costs of programs including personnel, space, time, registration, publicity, and materials | — | — | — |
| 26. | Plans cooperative programs with other professionals either from other library departments or community agencies and organizations | — | — | — |

# B-10 Physical Environment/Administration
## COLLECTION DEVELOPMENT

Date _____    Interviewer _____

Type of Interview (check one)    ☐ in person    ☐ phone    ☐ self-administered

Based on staff interviews, check **Yes**, **No**, or **No** Information regarding collection policies and practices. Refer to chapters 3 and 6 for descriptive information.

|  |  | Y | N | NI |
|---|---|---|---|---|
| 1. | The children's collection reflects a balanced proportion of circulating items for children, birth through age eight, based on the number of potential and actual users and in relationship to the total collection and acquisition budget for children's materials | — | — | — |
| 2. | General selection and acquisition policies ensure availability of pertinent materials for parents and children | — | — | — |
| 3. | Children are allowed to reserve and interloan materials | — | — | — |
| 4. | Materials are ordered on a planned, regularly scheduled basis using a variety of journals, catalogs, and reference sources | — | — | — |
| 5. | Materials are diversified to meet the needs of children who represent different populations and cultures, languages, gender, and abilities | — | — | — |
| 6. | Collections and displays promote awareness of different cultures | — | — | — |
| 7. | Materials are included that address the needs of children with disabilities, e.g., Braille books, large-print books, talking books, adaptive toys, assistive technology, access to a CCTV | — | — | — |
| 8. | Special kits provide an array of materials on specific topics including infancy and prenatal care, siblings, going to the hospital, death and dying, reading readiness skills, and children with special needs | — | — | — |
| 9. | Computers are available with appropriate software for preschool and primary grade children | — | — | — |
| 10. | Computers are available for parents to access electronic resources relevant to parenting and child rearing | — | — | — |
| 11. | Web sites are bookmarked for use by children and parents | — | — | — |
| 12. | Listening stations and appropriate audio materials are available for young children | — | — | — |
| 13. | Equipment and materials are organized to attract the interest of young children and promote independence | — | — | — |
| 14. | An ample amount of art supplies is available for programs and, if applicable, for use in the children's room | — | — | — |
| 15. | Manipulative materials, if available, include materials that focus on: sort and order, fit together and take apart, decode, and pretend with | — | — | — |
| 16. | Multiple copies of popular books and toys are available | — | — | — |
| 17. | Bibliographies related to parenting and child-rearing issues are regularly published and displayed | — | — | — |
| 18. | Bibliographies on materials available for young children are regularly published and displayed | — | — | — |
| 19. | Displays addressing parenting and child-rearing issues are available | — | — | — |

# B-11   Professional Development

Date _____   Interviewer _____

Based on staff interviews, check **R**arely, **S**ometimes, or **F**requently regarding the following practices. Refer to chapter 7 for descriptive information.

|     |                                                                                                                              | R | S | F |
|-----|------------------------------------------------------------------------------------------------------------------------------|---|---|---|
| 1.  | Provides and participates in ongoing staff development and training                                                          | — | — | — |
| 2.  | Keeps abreast of early childhood and family service literature                                                               | — | — | — |
| 3.  | Maintains a collection of children's materials for use in programs                                                           | — | — | — |
| 4.  | Maintains a professional collection for planning purposes and collection development                                         | — | — | — |
| 5.  | Serves on boards or committees of community, state, and national organizations                                               | — | — | — |
| 6.  | Conducts presentations on library services to boards, community groups, schools, and other organizations                     | — | — | — |
| 7.  | Trains support staff and volunteers to facilitate record keeping and communication among staff, families, and children       | — | — | — |
| 8.  | Trains staff and volunteers to create a responsive social environment                                                        | — | — | — |
| 9.  | Accesses in-service and continuing education opportunities to expand the range and scope of the library's service for young children and families | — | — | — |
| 10. | Conducts self-study on an ongoing basis                                                                                      | — | — | — |
| 11. | Implements performance or peer review with recommendation process                                                            | — | — | — |
| 12. | Represents the library in appropriate community networks                                                                      | — | — | — |

# B-12    Parent Focus Group

Date _____    Facilitator _____    Time: from _____ to _____

Element(s) _____

The questions below may also be used as part of an interview or survey.

## Introduction

Good evening and welcome to our session tonight. Thank you for taking the time to join our discussion of the library's parents' and children's services. We know and appreciate how valuable your time is. My name is Michelle Langa. I am an early childhood consultant. I was asked by the director, Mrs. Sandra Feinberg, to conduct these parent focus groups.

This is one of several meetings we are holding with parents who use the library's services. The purpose of this meeting is to get your input about services for parents and their children, birth through eight, as part of our Early Childhood Quality Review. We want to learn what you as a parent think about the types of services and programs you receive now. We also want to learn what you would like to see in the future. You have been selected because we trust your judgment. You are frequent users of the parent and children's sections of the library. We consider you our critical friends. We want to hear your ideas of how our parenting and children's services can improve.

Today's session will last a little over an hour. I will be taking notes and using a tape recorder in order not to miss any comments. We ask that you please speak up. Only one person should talk at a time. If several people are talking at a time the tape will get garbled and we may miss your important comments. I will combine your views with those from our other groups and summarize them in a report to the director and library board.

Let's begin. We've placed name cards in front of each of you to help us remember each other's names. Let's find out a little more about each other by going around the room one at a time. Please tell us your first name and how you heard about the library's parenting programs and early childhood services.

## Parenting Services

We will focus today (tonight) on library activities for you as a parent and those that you and your child use. We'll begin with library activities for parents.

1.  How have you used the library as a parent?

    *Probe:* Name a few of the services you have used in the past week or month.

2.  If you were to recommend the library's parenting programs to a friend, how would you describe them?

3.  How has the library helped you as a parent?

    *Probe:* Did you learn a valuable parenting tip or technique?

4.  Have you experienced any inconvenience or difficulties in using the library? The parenting series?

    *Probe:* Can you be more specific?

5.  Do you personally know someone in your neighborhood who does not use the library's parenting services?

    *Probe:* If so, have they shared with you the reasons why they do not use the library?

6.  As a parent, what other services would you like to see that do not exist presently?

7.  Do you feel you have a way to influence what parenting services are offered at the library?

8.  Has anyone ever suggested a topic for a parenting program?

    *Probe:* If not, are there reasons why you have not suggested a topic?

9.  Is there an area of the library that is uncomfortable for you to use as a parent?

(Continued)

## B-12   Parent Focus Group (continued)

### Children's Services

Now let's shift our focus to talking about library activities for parents and their young children.

1. Do you enjoy coming to the library with your child? Why?

   *Probe:* What are the activities that you and your child do at the library?

2. Does your child have a library card?

3. What are some of the things that your child has learned at the library?

4. Are there any rules or policies of the library that make it difficult for you and your child to use the library?

5. Is there an area of the library in which you or your child feels uncomfortable? comfortable?

### Library Staff

We would like to hear your views on the staff of the library.

1. Have you ever approached the librarians at the reference desk?

   *Probe:* What was that experience like for you?

2. How would you describe the librarians' attitudes toward parents?

3. What has been your experience when asking the staff for assistance?

   *Probe:* When was the last time you asked for assistance?

4. Do you feel comfortable when checking out materials at the circulation desk?

5. Would you go to a librarian with a suggestion for change?

   *Probe:* If you have already done so, what was that experience like for you?

6. Have you ever used a suggestion form?

### Suggestions for Improvement

We want to hear your opinions regarding ways to improve the library's services for parents and children.

1. What recommendations for improving the parents' and children's services of the library would you make?

2. This meeting has given us a lot of valuable information. Can you think of other ways parents can give us input?

3. If we were to plan more of these meetings in the future, would you be willing to attend?

### Closing Questions

We value the time you have given us today and want to ensure that you have had the opportunity to tell us what you think about the library's parents' and children's programs.

1. Have we missed anything?

2. Is there an area of discussion that you think we should have covered but did not?

3. *Summarize participants' comments in two or three sentences and ask:* Is this an accurate summary of what we discussed today?

(Continued)

## B-12   Parent Focus Group (continued)

### Note

Three focus groups were conducted at the Middle Country Public Library (Centereach, N.Y.), one of the field site libraries. Parents were contacted by staff and asked to participate in one-hour focus groups that would examine parenting and early childhood services as well as general staff responsiveness to patron comments and/or suggestions. The focus groups were conducted by Michelle Langa, a consultant hired by the library, and designed with input from the review team. This section outlines the introduction and the questions posed to participants. A tape recorder was used during the sessions.

A summary report of the comments that reflect the quality, staff attitude, and responsiveness to parents, user friendliness, and recommendations for change was provided to the children's department staff, administration, and board of trustees. This document provided further evidence about the library's practices and areas of strength and concern regarding service to parents and young children.

Parent Focus Groups, 1995. Conducted as part of the *Early Childhood Quality Review Initiative*. Centereach, N.Y.: Middle Country Public Library. © Reprinted by permission of Michelle Langa, MPA, CAS, Early Childhood Consultant, and the Middle Country Public Library

# C

## Observation
## Tools

# C-1  Observation Guide

Date _____  Observer _____  Time: from _____ to _____

Program/Service/Area _____

Age Level (check one)  parent/child:  ☐ infants  ☐ toddlers  ☐ preschool  ☐ K  ☐ elementary

child only:  ☐ preschool  ☐ K  ☐ elementary

other:  ☐ parents only  ☐ professional

When planning and conducting direct observations with running records or event sampling, consider the practices listed below.

## Scaffolding skill development

reference interview
discussion in story time
child's independent access to resources
sequential story time programming
child-size furniture
attention-span building
limit setting

## Validating self-motivated learning

introducing a range of resources
modeling for parents
working directly with the child
responding to the child's needs
providing parents with information about developmental issues
acknowledging child's actions and interests

## Encouraging intellectual risk taking

introducing new resources
issuing library card
offering materials not available at home
providing art and science activities for young children
displaying and integrating culturally diverse resources
nurturing a warm atmosphere
supporting a nonjudgmental environment

## Guiding exploration

program organization and management
layout of the library
reference and readers' advisory
independent access for children
extensive and diverse collections
age-appropriate software
interactive and interage learning opportunities
intergenerational programs
interdisciplinary approaches
resource centers

## Providing term for concepts and names for feelings

using and sharing literature
creating language-oriented activities and programs
labeling and organizing collections
developing collections that deal with emotional issues and family crises
including children with special needs
demonstrating acceptance of diversity
using gender-free language, illustrations, and displays

## Creating opportunities for discovery and creativity

hands-on activities
special displays or learner centers
developmentally and educationally appropriate programs
access to age-appropriate technology
material-rich environment
multicultural exhibits, displays, and collections
planned and safe environment

## Fostering emergent literacy

modeling reading and interest in books
offering opportunities for listening and following directions
introducing new vocabulary
encouraging remembering
sharing experiences
playing with language
guiding children to understand story lines
identifying characters
enhancing concept development
integrating ideas and experience
enjoying and showing interest in books
comparing word sounds and meanings
introducing numbers and letters
providing information on language and emergent literacy

## Problem solving and suggesting alternative approaches

active listening
resolution
choice of materials
educational software
Web searches
reference and readers' advisory
community referrals
interloans
parent education materials and programs
handouts for parents

## Creating varied opportunities to communicate

singing for and with children
talking and listening
modeling conflict-resolution strategies
reading interactive stories
demonstrating fingerplays
using manipulatives
introducing puppets
encouraging early peer social interaction
conducting reference interviews
providing summer reading programs
offering parent-child programs
developing interage programming
offering introductions to community networks
supporting parent-to-parent interactions
developing parent/professional partnerships

## Building self-esteem

giving kudos and warm fuzzies
acknowledging child to parent
displaying child's work
rewarding effort
recognizing individual achievement
encouraging questions

# C-2   Observing Children Working/Reviewing Children's Work

Date _____   Reviewer _____   Time: from _____ to _____

Program/Service/Area _____

Type of Review (check one)   ☐ direct observation   ☐ product review   ☐ other _____

Age Level (check one)   parent-child:   ☐ infants   ☐ toddlers   ☐ preschool   ☐ K   ☐ elementary

child only:   ☐ preschool   ☐ K   ☐ elementary

---

1. **In what kinds of activities are children engaged?**
   Consider multiple domains and developmental areas including: social, cognitive, information retrieval, language, manipulative (motor), emotional expression, and self-regulation.

2. **What skills are being learned?**
   Consider such skills as: following directions; making choices; matching and classification; fine motor coordination; large motor coordination; vocabulary building; semantic and pragmatic aspects of communication including but not limited to tone of voice, nonverbal behavior, forms of address and question asking, script and sequence; math (counting, time, one-on-one correspondence, simple arithmetic, logic); music (rhythm, melody).

3. **What kinds of resources are children utilizing?**
   Consider collections; data retrieval systems; services; staff; and physical aspects of the library environment such as tables and seating areas, signs and displays, books, computers, tapes and audio equipment, manipulatives.

4. **What are children producing and creating?**
   Describe the nature of the product and the range of individual creativity in multiple areas. Be sensitive to activities that offer children the opportunity to make choices and to express individuality.

(Continued)

## C-2    Observing Children Working/Reviewing Children's Work (continued)

5.  **What kinds of problem-solving challenges are children experiencing?**
    Problem solving for young children takes many forms in the physical and social realm including but not limited to: planning, sharing resources, waiting, controlling emotions (self-control), taking responsibility, recognizing, matching, selecting (choosing), ordering, prioritizing, decision making, expressing ideas.

6.  **What modeling is taking place for parents/caregivers/children by librarians and library staff?**
    Consideration should be given to multiple areas including but not limited to appropriateness of activities, offering choices, setting limits, redirecting, using positive language, acknowledging child, listening, responding calmly, participating actively, scaffolding, resolving conflicts, using positive discipline, strategies for handling transitions, recognizing emergent literacy skills.

7.  **What kinds of inferences can you make about the quality of learning these children are experiencing?**
    Consider the importance of children's acquisition of attitudes and feelings toward learning, the self as a learner, the library setting, emotional learning, curiosity about materials and ideas, attempting mastery of specific concepts, perseverance, experimentation, practicing specific skills.

8.  **Keeping in mind what you observe, are there any surprises or concerns?**
    Concepts such as the social embeddedness of learning, the contextual aspects of learning, and the zone of proximal development may be of assistance in reviewing the creation of a learning environment for young children.

*This form may be used individually or for group discussions.*

## C-3  Social Environment/Professional Development/ Parent Participation

Date _____  Observer _____  Time: from _____ to _____

Program/Children's Area _____

When observing staff in the children's room or in a children's program, check **R**arely, **S**ometimes, **F**requently, or **N**ot **O**bserved regarding the behaviors listed. Refer to chapter 2 for descriptions of appropriate behaviors.

| **Communication and Engagement** | **R** | **S** | **F** | **NO** |
|---|---|---|---|---|
| 1.  Greets children warmly | — | — | — | — |
| 2.  Greets adults warmly | — | — | — | — |
| 3.  Interacts with children regularly | — | — | — | — |
| 4.  Interacts at eye level whenever possible | — | — | — | — |
| 5.  Models positive social interaction, warmth, affection, and gentle appropriate touching | — | — | — | — |
| 6.  Listens to children with respect and reflects ideas/feelings behind children's words and behavior | — | — | — | — |
| 7.  Listens to adults with respect and uses reflective communication techniques | — | — | — | — |
| 8.  Elicits communication from children using developmentally appropriate techniques | — | — | — | — |
| 9.  Uses positive statements | — | — | — | — |
| 10.  Avoids negative verbalizations | — | — | — | — |
| 11.  Uses language free of stereotyping phrases and labels | — | — | — | — |
| 12.  Exhibits awareness of language use and developmental level of each child | — | — | — | — |
| 13.  Facilitates language learning by encouraging children to express feelings with words | — | — | — | — |
| 14.  Recognizes differing moods of children and adjusts standards for them when they are fatigued, irritated, or overstimulated | — | — | — | — |
| 15.  Respects ethnic differences | — | — | — | — |

| **Modeling and Facilitating** | | | | |
|---|---|---|---|---|
| 16.  Focuses on individual children while being aware of what is happening throughout the room | — | — | — | — |
| 17.  Focuses on behavior without labeling child | — | — | — | — |
| 18.  Models appropriate behavior for children | — | — | — | — |
| 19.  Models appropriate behavior for adults | — | — | — | — |
| 20.  Attends promptly to children in need of assistance | — | — | — | — |

(Continued)

## C-3   Social Environment/Professional Development/Parent Participation (continued)

|  |  | R | S | F | NO |
|---|---|---|---|---|---|
| 21. | Offers children choices of activities/materials | — | — | — | — |
| 22. | Encourages children's decision making | — | — | — | — |
| 23. | Exhibits willingness to follow children's lead | — | — | — | — |
| 24. | Engages children in activities that enhance language understanding and use | — | — | — | — |
| 25. | Conveys sense of pleasure in interaction with children | — | — | — | — |
| 26. | Shows appreciation for children's creative answers and observations | — | — | — | — |
| 27. | Talks to children about activities in which they are involved | — | — | — | — |
| 28. | Talks to parents about activities in which they are involved | — | — | — | — |
| 29. | Shares humorous incidents with children and parents | — | — | — | — |
| 30. | Talks to children about books they are reading | — | — | — | — |
| 31. | Talks to parents about books they are reading | — | — | — | — |
| 32. | Encourages children to use whole body and multiple senses | — | — | — | — |
| 33. | Encourages physical exploration and manipulation of objects | — | — | — | — |
| 34. | Encourages parent/caregiver to interact and play with children | — | — | — | — |
| 35. | Shows appreciation for children's play | — | — | — | — |
| 36. | Models appropriate play activities | — | — | — | — |
| 37. | Acknowledges when children initiate their own play activities | — | — | — | — |
| 38. | Scaffolds children's independent behaviors | — | — | — | — |
| 39. | Facilitates interaction among children | — | — | — | — |
| 40. | Fosters cooperation and other prosocial behaviors among children | | | | |

### Management and Supervision

|  |  | R | S | F | NO |
|---|---|---|---|---|---|
| | | — | — | — | — |
| 41. | Supervises carefully and intervenes to avoid problems | — | — | — | — |
| 42. | Responds to children's bids for attention | — | — | — | — |
| 43. | Responds quickly to children's behavior that compromises their safety or the safety of others | — | — | — | — |
| | | — | — | — | — |
| 44. | Provides consistent, clear expectations that are demonstrated or explained to children | — | — | — | — |
| 45. | Sets consistent, realistic limits with children | — | — | — | — |
| 46. | Discusses a child's behavior with parent only when child is absent | — | — | — | — |
| 47. | Uses calm voice and remains in control in difficult situations | — | — | — | — |

(Continued)

## C-3   Social Environment/Professional Development/Parent Participation   (continued)

|  | R | S | F | NO |
|---|---|---|---|---|
| **Staff Interactions** | — | — | — | — |
| 48.  Is positive and expresses a feeling of warmth and support | — | — | — | — |
| 49.  Avoids discussing children's behavior publicly with staff or other adults | — | — | — | — |
| 50.  Provides on-floor training to new librarians | — | — | — | — |
| 51.  Asks for help when needed | — | — | — | — |
| 52.  Expresses approval and support for other staff | — | — | — | — |
| 53.  Is aware of other librarians' needs and takes over when necessary | — | — | — | — |
| 54.  Makes independent decisions when necessary | — | — | — | — |

Comments:

## C-4  Social Environment/Professional Development/ Parent Participation

Date _____     Observer _____     Time: from _____ to _____

When observing staff in the children's room, check **R**arely, **S**ometimes, **F**requently, or **N**ot **O**bserved regarding the behaviors listed. Refer to chapter 2 for descriptions of appropriate behaviors.

|  |  | R | S | F | NO |
|---|---|---|---|---|---|
| 1. | Positions self and desk area strategically for viewing room | ___ | ___ | ___ | ___ |
| 2. | Encourages social interactions | ___ | ___ | ___ | ___ |
| 3. | Is readily available to patrons | ___ | ___ | ___ | ___ |
| 4. | Assists children promptly with books, materials, computers, and equipment | ___ | ___ | ___ | ___ |
| 5. | Assists adults promptly with books, materials, computers, and equipment | ___ | ___ | ___ | ___ |
| 6. | Communicates with parents at children's reference desk | ___ | ___ | ___ | ___ |
| 7. | Communicates with parents in children's room | ___ | ___ | ___ | ___ |
| 8. | Walks around room seeking children or adults who may need assistance | ___ | ___ | ___ | ___ |
| 9. | Engages children in the reference review | ___ | ___ | ___ | ___ |
| 10. | Engages adults in the reference review | ___ | ___ | ___ | ___ |
| 11. | Offers follow-up assistance after the first interaction | ___ | ___ | ___ | ___ |

Comments:

## C-5   Social Environment/Professional Development/ Parent Participation

Date _____   Observer _____   Time: from _____ to _____

Program _____

When observing staff in a children's program, check **R**arely, **S**ometimes, **F**requently, or **N**ot **O**bserved regarding the behaviors listed. Refer to chapter 2 for descriptions of appropriate behaviors.

| | R | S | F | NO |
|---|---|---|---|---|
| 1. Greets children by name | — | — | — | — |
| 2. Is aware of and adjusts to differing moods of children | — | — | — | — |
| 3. Shows enthusiasm for program | — | — | — | — |
| 4. Reads/sings with feeling and expression | — | — | — | — |
| 5. Encourages children to recognize their experiences and understand concepts | — | — | — | — |
| 6. Uses materials that reflect cultural and ethnic diversity | — | — | — | — |
| 7. Uses materials that show a range of family configurations | — | — | — | — |
| 8. Uses materials and activities appropriate for developmental level of participants | — | — | — | — |
| 9. Uses materials that are safe and durable | — | — | — | — |
| 10. Provides multiple copies of books and materials for children to use | — | — | — | — |
| 11. Plans and implements a comfortable departure | — | — | — | — |
| 12. Effectively handles separation problems when necessary | — | — | — | — |
| 13. Speaks with parents before program | — | — | — | — |
| 14. Speaks with parents after program | — | — | — | — |
| 15. Speaks with parents during parent-child program | — | — | — | — |
| 16. Demonstrates appropriate group management skills | — | — | — | — |
| 17. Provides materials to assist parents/caregivers in extending the activities at home | — | — | — | — |
| 18. Provides circulating materials for children | — | — | — | — |

Comments:

# C-6   Physical Environment/Administration

Date _____   Observer _____   Time: from _____ to _____

When observing in the children's room check **Y**es, **N**o, or **N**eeds **I**mprovement regarding the environment. Refer to chapter 3 for descriptive information.

| **Organization of Early Childhood Area** | **Y** | **N** | **NI** |
|---|---|---|---|
| 1.  Organization of the environment is clear | — | — | — |
| 2.  Activity and learning centers are easily recognizable (materials with similar use or themes grouped together) | — | — | — |
| 3.  Activity centers contain things that can be touched or manipulated | — | — | — |
| 4.  Activity areas provide space for children and adults to stand, sit, or work next to each other | — | — | — |
| 5.  Activity areas provide space for young children to move, practice large motor activities, and learn with entire body | — | — | — |
| 6.  Young children can access a portion of collections (books, materials, and manipulatives/toys) without adult assistance | — | — | — |
| 7.  Low shelves, open bins (without lids or covers), and/or low hooks or hangers hold materials that children can access themselves | — | — | — |
| 8.  Furniture and seating is available for small groups of two to four people to gather in face-to-face interactions | — | — | — |
| 9.  Quiet and noisy activities are separated | — | — | — |
| 10.  Activity centers can been seen with unobstructed views from more than one section in the children's area | — | — | — |
| 11.  A separate room is available for special programs | — | — | — |
| 12.  Noise levels are minimized by design considerations | — | — | — |
| 13.  Lighting, including windows and natural lighting, enhances the environment | — | — | — |
| **Accommodations for Range of Ages and Families** | | | |
| 14.  Strollers and carriages can be accommodated | — | — | — |
| 15.  If there is a railing, stairs, or playpen, the railings meet acceptable standards | — | — | — |
| 16.  An area for infants is available | — | — | — |
| 17.  Materials with small parts that could be ingested are stored out of reach of infants and toddlers | — | — | — |
| 18.  Furniture scaled to the needs of young children is adequate to meet demand | — | — | — |
| 19.  An area with soft furnishings for adults and children to share is available | — | — | — |

(Continued)

## C-6  Physical Environment/Administration  (continued)

|  | Y | N | NI |
|---|---|---|---|
| 20. Adult size chairs for parents/caregivers are available | — | — | — |
| 21. Separate places to put equipment and outerwear are available | — | — | — |

### Reference Area

| | Y | N | NI |
|---|---|---|---|
| 22. Reference desk near young children's area has a lowered section to allow for four- to eight-year-olds to see over top | — | — | — |
| 23. Reference desk near young children's area has a space for adults to rest materials out of reach of young children | — | — | — |
| 24. Information about programs, services, and special collections for young children and their families is visible and accessible | — | — | — |
| 25. Information about behavior limits and responsibilities of patrons, both adult and children, is clearly visible | — | — | — |
| 26. Activity centers for young children are visible from reference desk | — | — | — |

### Displays

| | Y | N | NI |
|---|---|---|---|
| 27. Sense of family place and messages of welcome are established through use of design features and/or hanging decorations and displays | — | — | — |
| 28. Color, light, and design elements are used to create cheerful decorations of interest | — | — | — |
| 29. Displays/decorations are free of gender stereotypes | — | — | — |
| 30. Displays, exhibits, and activity/learning areas are of interest to young children | — | — | — |
| 30. Displays, exhibits, and informational/learning areas of interest to parents/caregivers are located within or adjacent to areas for young children | — | — | — |
| 31. Displays, exhibits, and interest areas encourage recognition of symbols, letters, and numbers | — | — | — |
| 32. Pictorial symbols and letters are used to assist in communicating organization of area | — | — | — |
| 33. Displays, exhibits, and interest areas encourage ethnic pride and the recognition of cultural diversity | — | — | — |
| 34. Children's projects and artwork are displayed | — | — | — |
| 35. Children's projects and artwork are displayed at eye level for young children | — | — | — |
| 36. Displays are made of low-flammable material | — | — | — |

Comments:

# C-7  Parent Participation/Professional Development

Date _____      Observer _____      Time: from _____ to _____

Program/Children's Area _____

When observing staff in the children's room or in a children's or parents' program, check **R**arely, **S**ometimes, **F**requently, or **N**ot **O**bserved regarding the behaviors listed.  Refer to chapter 4 for descriptions of appropriate behaviors..

|  | R | S | F | NO |
|---|---|---|---|---|
| 1. Talks regularly with parents before, during, and after each program | — | — | — | — |
| 2. Supports and encourages parent-child interactions that are appropriate for the child's developmental level and are mutually enjoyable | — | — | — | — |
| 3. Responds appropriately to families' need for information and support | — | — | — | — |
| 4. Assists parents and other adult family members in making independent decisions | — | — | — | — |
| 5. Welcomes parent input on child's participation in library activity | — | — | — | — |
| 6. Welcomes parent input on learning that has occurred as a result of a library experience | — | — | — | — |
| 7. Models appropriate teaching and limit-setting techniques for parents to use in the home environment | — | — | — | — |
| 8. Provides parents with specific information on their child's participation in the library setting | — | — | — | — |
| 9. Encourages parents to check out materials for child | — | — | — | — |
| 10. Is familiar with parenting materials and consistently offers appropriate materials upon request | — | — | — | — |
| 11. Encourages parents to check out materials for themselves | — | — | — | — |
| 12. Encourages parents to serve as resource people in children's programs | — | — | — | — |
| 13. Encourages parents to serve as resource people in programs for parents and other family members | — | — | — | — |

Comments:

# D

# Documentation
# Examination Tools

Library Portfolio Checklist
**D-1**

Library Portfolio Questions
**D-2**

Document Analysis Questions
**D-3**

Physical Environment/Administration Checklist
**D-4**

Parent Participation/Collaborations Checklist
**D-5**

Parent Participation/Collaborations/Administration Checklist
**D-6**

Collaborations/Administration Checklist
**D-7**

Collaborations/Administration Checklist (Professional Collection)
**D-8**

Administration Checklist
**D-9**

Professional Development Checklist
**D-10**

# D-1  Library Portfolio

Date _____     Reviewer _____

The portfolio could include a brief summary (maximum of one page) of each of the following or the materials can be collected and displayed in their original format. Check **A**vailable, **N**ot **A**vailable, or **C**reated for **R**eview. Using forms D-2 and D-3, analyze the documents collected.

|  | A | NA | CR |
|---|---|---|---|
| 1. The mission statement | — | — | — |
| 2. Community demographics of the library service area that particularly focus on young children and families | — | — | — |
| 3. Documentation of health and safety compliance with regard to children's areas | — | — | — |
| 4. Materials on youth or parent advisory committees, user surveys, patron focus groups, or other activities that reflect patron participation in children's services | — | — | — |
| 5. Descriptive materials on: | | | |
|    a. The children's and parent/professional collections, including adaptive and special materials | — | — | — |
|    b. Programs for children (birth through eight years), parents, and professionals who work with families | — | — | — |
|    c. Special areas/sections of the children's room | — | — | — |
|    d. Outreach services | — | — | — |
|    e. Integration of technology | — | — | — |
|    f. Community directories or databases | — | — | — |
| 6. Library publications including bibliographies and brochures that focus on this particular clientele | — | — | — |
| 7. Flyers, program notices, and written procedures | — | — | — |
| 8. Children's projects | — | — | — |
| 9. Library policies: | | | |
|    a. Library-card registration, particularly age of eligibility, responsibility, and parent/caregiver involvement | — | — | — |
|    b. Confidentiality | — | — | — |
|    c. Free access to information for minors | — | — | — |
|    d. Use of technology and Internet access | — | — | — |
|    e. Community access to meeting rooms, bulletin boards or display areas | — | — | — |
|    f. Fines and fees | — | — | — |
|    g. Access to equipment | — | — | — |
|    h. Circulation, particularly the issues of renewals, reserves, interlibrary loans, and nonbook materials | — | — | — |

(Continued)

## D-1  Library Portfolio  (continued)

|  | A | NA | CR |
|---|---|---|---|
| i. Reference and program services including homework assistance, telephone reference responses, and registration procedures |  |  |  |
| j. Photocopying | — | — | — |
| k. Unattended children | — | — | — |
| l. Behavior standards and limits | — | — | — |
| m. Hours of service | — | — | — |
| n. Cleaning and safety | — | — | — |
| 10. Schedules, program assignments, job descriptions, procedure manuals, organizational charts, staff development activities, and other management materials | — | — | — |
| 11. Partnerships with parents, local schools and other educational institutions, community-based organizations, the corporate community, and social and health organizations | — | — | — |
| 12. Other | — | — | — |
|  | — | — | — |

Additional materials may be gathered by the review team members and integrated into the portfolio throughout the review period.

# D-2  Library Portfolio

Date _____     Reviewer _____

Review the portfolio material using form D-3. Summarize your analysis using the questions below.

What information does the portfolio provide regarding the library's service to young children and parents?

What are some of the strengths about services for young children displayed in the portfolio? Does the portfolio reflect evidence of better practice?

What are some of the concerns or areas of reflection about service for young children presented in the portfolio?

What recommendations can be made after viewing the portfolio?

What additional materials need to be collected?

# D-3   Document Analysis

Date _____     Reviewer _____

Type of document(s) _____

Source: (check one)   ☐ internal    ☐ external

Annotation:

How does this document(s) provide evidence of support for early childhood service?

What are the areas of reflection or concern that are identified after examining this document(s)?

What recommendations can be made after reviewing the document(s)?

# D-4   Physical Environment/Administration  CHILDREN'S COLLECTION

Date _____     Reviewer _____

Using the catalog and staff interviews, consider availability and condition of the children's collection. Check all that apply: **A**vailable, **N**ot **A**vailable, **I**n-house, **C**irculation, **AD**equate, **N**eeds **I**mprovement.

| | A | NA | I | C | AD | NI |
|---|---|---|---|---|---|---|
| Books of various types (board, cloth, oversized) | — | — | — | — | — | — |
| Books for infants and toddlers | — | — | — | — | — | — |
| Books for preschoolers | — | — | — | — | — | — |
| Books for primary grade students | — | — | — | — | — | — |
| Talking books | — | — | — | — | — | — |
| Braille books | — | — | — | — | — | — |
| Computer stations | — | — | — | — | — | — |
| Web sites targeted to children | — | — | — | — | — | — |
| Computer software for preschoolers | — | — | — | — | — | — |
| Computer software for primary grade children | — | — | — | — | — | — |
| Assistive technology | — | — | — | — | — | — |
| Multimedia stations | — | — | — | — | — | — |
| Videos for preschoolers | — | — | — | — | — | — |
| Videos for primary grade children | — | — | — | — | — | — |
| Compact discs, records, and/or cassettes for preschoolers | — | — | — | — | — | — |
| Compact discs, records, and/or cassettes for primary grade children | — | — | — | — | — | — |
| Multimedia kits | — | — | — | — | — | — |
| Toys | — | — | — | — | — | — |
| Adaptive toys | — | — | — | — | — | — |
| Puzzles and pegboards | — | — | — | — | — | — |
| Art supplies | — | — | — | — | — | — |
| Blocks and building materials | — | — | — | — | — | — |
| Science equipment, e.g., magnifying glass, wall charts, posters, weights | — | — | — | — | — | — |
| Active play equipment, e.g., climbing equipment, wheel toys, sand/water table | — | — | — | — | — | — |
| Manipulatives to sort, classify, and label | | | | | | |
| Dramatic play equipment or materials, e.g., dress-up items, dollhouse, puppet stage puppets and dolls, flannelboard | — | — | — | — | — | — |
| | — | — | — | — | — | — |
| CCTV | — | — | — | — | — | — |

Briefly describe other collections that are appropriate and available for young children:

# D-5 Parent Participation/Collaborations

Date _____ Reviewer _____

When reviewing documents and written materials, check **R**arely, **S**ometimes, **F**requently, or **N**o **I**nformation regarding the practices listed. Refer to chapter 4 for background description.

|  | R | S | F | NI |
|---|---|---|---|---|
| 1. Individual programs and collections include a written description of the program's philosophy and operating procedures | — | — | — | — |
| 2. Parents are invited to participate in early childhood programs | — | — | — | — |
| 3. Parents provide input through the use of focus groups, an advisory council, suggestion boxes, or surveys | — | — | — | — |
| 4. Parent-education programs are offered for parents | — | — | — | — |
| 5. Parent and early childhood programs have a program evaluation component | — | — | — | — |
| 6. Information on early childhood services is available in alternative formats or languages as needed | — | — | — | — |
| 7. Information for parents is posted or displayed in the library | — | — | — | — |
| 8. Programs are offered in a parent's home language or translators are available as needed to facilitate parent participation | — | — | — | — |
| 9. Alternative forms of communication and participation are available for parents with disabilities | — | — | — | — |

# D-6  Parent Participation/Collaborations/Administration
## PARENTS' COLLECTION

Date _____    Reviewer _____

Using the catalog and staff interviews, consider availability and condition of the parents' collection. Check all that apply: **A**vailable, **N**ot **A**vailable, **I**n-house, **C**irculation, **AD**equate, **N**eeds **I**mprovement.

| Types of Materials | A | NA | I | C | AD | NI |
|---|---|---|---|---|---|---|
| Reference materials | — | — | — | — | — | — |
| Books | — | — | — | — | — | — |
| Periodicals | — | — | — | — | — | — |
| Videos | — | — | — | — | — | — |
| Newsletters | — | — | — | — | — | — |
| Pamphlets | — | — | — | — | — | — |
| Audiocassettes | — | — | — | — | — | — |
| Computer software | — | — | — | — | — | — |
| Web sites targeted to parents | — | — | — | — | — | — |
| Specially designed kits | — | — | — | — | — | — |

| Topics Covered | | | | | | |
|---|---|---|---|---|---|---|
| Child development (cognitive language, physical, and emotional) | — | — | — | — | — | — |
| Common childhood illnesses | — | — | — | — | — | — |
| Discipline and parenting skills | — | — | — | — | — | — |
| Infant care and child-rearing guidance | — | — | — | — | — | — |
| Language and reading activities | — | — | — | — | — | — |
| Nutrition and physical fitness | — | — | — | — | — | — |
| Speech and language development | — | — | — | — | — | — |
| Children's fears | — | — | — | — | — | — |
| Toilet training | — | — | — | — | — | — |
| Home schooling | — | — | — | — | — | — |
| Sleep problems | — | — | — | — | — | — |
| Emotional disorders of childhood | — | — | — | — | — | — |
| Children and the media | — | — | — | — | — | — |
| Death and bereavement | — | — | — | — | — | — |

(Continued)

## D-6  Parent Participation/Collaborations/Administration
### PARENT'S COLLECTION  (continued)

| Topics Covered *continued* | A | NA | I | C | AD | NI |
|---|---|---|---|---|---|---|
| Home and school issues | — | — | — | — | — | — |
| Working parents | — | — | — | — | — | — |
| Developmentally appropriate activities for children | — | — | — | — | — | — |
| Divorce, single-parent, gay family, and stepfamily issues | — | — | — | — | — | — |
| Communication and family relationships | — | — | — | — | — | — |
| Family travel and recreation | — | — | — | — | — | — |
| Safety and health | — | — | — | — | — | — |
| Parenting children with special needs | — | — | — | — | — | — |
| Sibling relationships | — | — | — | — | — | — |
| Pregnancy and prenatal care | — | — | — | — | — | — |
| Stress and depression in children | — | — | — | — | — | — |
| Sexuality education | — | — | — | — | — | — |
| Children's parties | — | — | — | — | — | — |
| Children's toys, furniture, rooms, and equipment | — | — | — | — | — | — |
| Adolescent issues | — | — | — | — | — | — |
| Child abuse and family dysfunction | — | — | — | — | — | — |
| Adoption and foster care | — | — | — | — | — | — |
| Alcohol and substance abuse | | | | | | |
| Specific health and disability topics | | | | | | |

Briefly describe other collections that are appropriate and available for parents.

Briefly describe other topics that are appropriate and available for  parents.

# D-7  Collaborations/Administration

Date _____      Reviewer _____

Check **A**vailable, **N**ot **A**vailable, or **C**reated for **R**eview for each type of documentation listed. Use form D-3 to analyze the documents.

|  | A | NA | CR |
|---|---|---|---|
| 1. Meetings, training sessions, and conferences attended by children's staff during the past three years | — | — | — |
| 2. List of committees and organizations in which staff participates | — | — | — |
| 3. Agreements and contracts between the library and community agencies or organizations | — | — | — |
| 4. Rolodex files and phone logs of children's staff | — | — | — |
| 5. Grant proposals, those funded and not funded, that include partnerships with other organizations | — | — | — |
| 6. Directory or listing of library programs and services for young children and families | — | — | — |
| 7. Guidelines and procedures for the distribution of library flyers and brochures | — | — | — |
| 8. Guidelines and procedures for the distribution of community brochures through the children's department | — | — | — |

Other:

# D-8   Collaborations/Administration   PROFESSIONAL COLLECTION

Date _____   Reviewer _____

Using the catalog and staff interviews, consider availability and condition of the professional collection. Check all that apply: **A**vailable, **N**ot **A**vailable, **I**n-house, **C**irculation, **AD**equate, **N**eeds **I**mprovement.

| Types of Materials | A | NA | I | C | AD | NI |
|---|---|---|---|---|---|---|
| Reference materials | — | — | — | — | — | — |
| Books | — | — | — | — | — | — |
| Periodicals | — | — | — | — | — | — |
| Videos | — | — | — | — | — | — |
| Newsletters | — | — | — | — | — | — |
| Pamphlets | — | — | — | — | — | — |
| Audiocassettes | — | — | — | — | — | — |
| Computer software | — | — | — | — | — | — |
| Web sites targeted to professionals | — | — | — | — | — | — |
| Specially designed kits | — | — | — | — | — | — |

| Topics Covered | | | | | | |
|---|---|---|---|---|---|---|
| Developmentally appropriate environments and activities | — | — | — | — | — | — |
| Parent/teacher communications | — | — | — | — | — | — |
| Early childhood curriculum materials | — | — | — | — | — | — |
| Art and recreational activities | — | — | — | — | — | — |
| Creative movement and music activities | — | — | — | — | — | — |
| Parent-education programs and curricula | — | — | — | — | — | — |
| Resource guides to children's books and related activities | — | — | — | — | — | — |
| Classroom-management and discipline techniques | — | — | — | — | — | — |
| Working with pregnant and parenting teens | — | — | — | — | — | — |
| Family-centered care | — | — | — | — | — | — |
| Conflict resolution and multicultural education | — | — | — | — | — | — |
| Model family support programs and services | — | — | — | — | — | — |
| Child-care management and training | — | — | — | — | — | — |
| Working with culturally diverse audiences | — | — | — | — | — | — |
| Working with diverse family structures | — | — | — | — | — | — |
| Child abuse, neglect, and family dysfunction | — | — | — | — | — | — |

Briefly describe other collections or topics that are appropriate and available for family-support professionals.

# D-9  Administration

Date _____  Reviewer _____

Check **A**vailable, **N**ot **A**vailable, or **C**reated for **R**eview for each type of documentation listed. Use form D–3 to analyze the documents.

| | A | NA | CR |
|---|---|---|---|
| **Community Data** | | | |
| 1. A community needs assessment within the library's service area | — | — | — |
| 2. A demographic profile of the community particularly noting patterns of young children birth through eight years | — | — | — |
| 3. Information on ethnicity, income, and household status relative to families with young children | — | — | — |
| 4. Data regarding the education, health, nutrition, and social service needs of children and their families | — | — | — |
| 5. Information on family and early childhood resources available in the community | — | — | — |
| 6. School district data | — | — | — |
| **Library Data** | | | |
| 7. The library's long-range or strategic plan | — | — | — |
| 8. Reports on focus groups, surveys, evaluations, etc., conducted during the past five years | — | — | — |
| 9. Library policies and procedures developed for public service including registration, confidentiality, access, fines, fees, reference, interloan, etc. | — | — | — |
| 10. Health, hygiene, and safety policies and procedures | — | — | — |
| 11. A directory or list of library programs, services, and collections aimed at young children, families, and adults who work with families | — | — | — |
| 12. Schedules that reflect reference desk, planning, and programming activities | — | — | — |
| 13. Written program procedures, record-keeping procedures, statistical and survey forms, brochures, flyers, directories, bibliographies, guidelines, and other pieces of the library's internal and external communications system | — | — | — |
| 14. Program and collection analysis, particularly about material use by young children and their families | — | — | — |
| 15. Record of recruitment efforts for volunteers and of volunteer orientation and training | — | — | — |
| 16. Salaries relative to those of adult services staff | — | — | — |
| 17. Institutional chain of command; reporting hierarchy for children's services staff | — | — | — |
| 18. Other: | | | |

*Refer to form D-10 for further types of documentation.*

# D-10   Professional Development

Date _____   Reviewer _____

Check **A**vailable, **N**ot **A**vailable, or **C**reated for **R**eview for each type of documentation listed.  Use form D–3 to analyze the documents.

|  |  | A | NA | CR |
|---|---|---|---|---|
| 1. | Performance evaluations, job descriptions, qualifications and resumes, education and training experience of children's services staff | —— | —— | —— |
| 2. | Documents reflecting conference attendance, participation on boards and committees, commitments to professional organizations | —— | —— | —— |
| 3. | Staff publications including books, articles, bibliographies, bookmarks, publicity materials, program materials, newsletters, brochures, exhibits, displays, etc. | —— | —— | —— |
| 4. | A list of continuing education activities during the past several years | —— | —— | —— |
| 5. | Subscriptions to professional journals and publications | —— | —— | —— |
| 6. | Records on the use of volunteers | —— | —— | —— |

# INDEX

**Sandra Feinberg,** Director of the Middle Country Public Library, has devoted the past twenty-five years to public library service, fifteen of them to the development of children's services. A passionate believer in the ability of public libraries to be family-oriented community institutions, she has been a front-runner in the development of innovative programs and services for children and parents. Her accomplishments include the creation of the Parent/Child Workshop and the design of a 12,000-square-foot children's room that contains an early childhood area, a parent's collection, a reading garden, two computer areas, and a museum for children. She is the coauthor of five books on Children's librarianship and family services, including *The Early Childhood Quality Review Initiative for Public Libraries,* a grant-funded project publication that served as a framework for this publication. She is currently an adjunct professor at the Palmer School of Library and Information Science, Long Island University.

**Joan Kuchner,** Ph.D., Acting Director of Child and Family Studies, State University of New York (SUNY) at Stony Brook, received her doctorate in psychology from the University of Chicago where she focused on infancy, early childhood, and cross-cultural parent-child relationships. She is presently a full-time faculty member of SUNY at Stony Brook's Social Science Interdisciplinary Program, teaching courses on human development, early childhood environments, the infant and young child, children's play, and children, law, and social policy. *The Health Policy Manual* and *The Student Handbook* for Child Care Services were published under her editorial supervision. She has twice received SUNY at Stony Brook's Diversity Award for her educational outreach programs. Dr. Kuchner serves on community boards and is a frequent presenter at professional conferences. She has contributed to several books on the psychology of women and served as a consultant to *The Early Childhood Quality Review Initiative for Public Libraries.*

**Sari Feldman** became the Head of Community Services for the Cleveland Public Library in 1997. In that capacity she oversees the twenty-eight neighborhood libraries in the city of Cleveland, the Library for the Blind and Physically Handicapped, and the development of family literacy services. During her fourteen-year tenure at the Onondaga County Public Library she developed a number of early childhood and family services including Ready, Set, Read and PIRL (Parent Information Resource Library). Feldman is also an adjunct faculty member of the Syracuse University School of Information Studies. She has received both the University Vice President's Award for the Teacher of the Year and the School of Information Studies Innovation in Community Service Award. Feldman has presented numerous workshops and lectures and has written for professional journals. She is the co-author of several books, including *The Early Childhood Quality Review Initiative for Public Libraries,* a grant-funded project publication that served as a framework for this book.